Do you know what "Potato Salad Time" is? When you read Mike Huckabee's compelling message *Rare, Medium or Done Well: Make the Most of Your Life* you will! And although I pretty much disagree with all of Mike Huckabee's political views, you might be shocked to learn that this book is one I actually endorse! Set aside your political passions long enough to enjoy an uplifting call to think bigger than the things that divide us. We may have big differences, but Mike's book proves we agree on things that matter.

—**Van Jones**, CNN News Host & Political Commentator

Only my Southern-Fried Friend Mike Huckabee would title a book chapter "Potato Salad Time." If you don't know what that means, you probably grew up someplace where grits aren't on the menu either! This book is worth buying and reading just to learn how important it is to be ready for YOUR "Potato Salad Time."

—**Todd Starnes**, Fox News and Fox News Radio
and Best-Selling Author

I am drawn to books that have been written from a person's "insides." This is just that book. The author is well-known, so many of us are already familiar with his politics, the members of his family, even his spiritual beliefs . . . but what does Mike Huckabee *really* think about when he is alone? What does *he* know about the future of *my* family? If I paid for the time and provided the pen and ink, what could—what *would*—a wise man tell me about myself? Stated simply . . . *Rare, Medium or Done Well* is the book you and I have been waiting for someone—*anyone*—to write. Now Mike Huckabee has done it. Mom, dad, teenager, grandparent, young adult . . . do you want to "Make the Most of Your Life?" Yep. Me, too. Read this book. I'm about to start it again.

—**Andy Andrews**, *New York Times* Best-Selling Author
of *The Traveler's Gift* and *The Noticer*

Here's a sobering thought by a comedian: "we die a little every day." Know how to counter that? Get busy living and living well. You'll need a guide and THIS book is perfect. Thank you, Governor!

—**Chonda Pierce**, Comedian

Life is not a dress rehearsal—and there are no re-takes. Our friend Mike Huckabee vividly brings that message home in his provocative book *Rare, Medium or Done Well*. Using his trademark humor and acerbic wit, he champions the sobering lesson of preparing for the final curtain-call.

—**Kevin and Sam Sorbo**, Filmmakers

I've known Mike Huckabee since 1991, before his first political race. We've been friends since and I've watched him through campaigns, holding the offices of Lt. Governor and Governor in Arkansas, campaigns for President, a successful career in television, radio, and as a bestselling author. He's had many roles, but one thing has been consistent and constant—his focus on the FINAL chapter of his life. His message in this book can be embraced and loved by people on the left or right, but especially by those who know that our most important direction at the end of life is UP!"

—**Ralph Reed**, Christian Activist, Author, Political Strategist

When you look at life's menu and see "Mike Huckabee" just order it well done . . . for those are the words that describe his own life and legacy. I love the message of this new book—read it and reap!

—**O.S. Hawkins**, Author of *The Joshua Code* and
the Code Series devotionals and
President/CEO of GuideStone Financial Resources

There is little more a father (or parents) can ever do than build and leave legacy for, with, and in their children. Not a material legacy, but a legacy of substance. Governor Mike Huckabee's timely emphasis could not correspond with greater need than the vacuum that today's culture presents.

—**Kevin McCullough**, "Binge Thinker", PM Drive Host:
Salem Media Group

My friendship with Governor Huckabee continues to enrich my life with a deep understanding of life, faith, and the importance of building and keeping a spiritual base within my family. This book will enrich the life of everyone who reads this most wonderful book. Thank you, Governor Huckabee!

—**Tony Orlando**, Singer

Mike Huckabee and I shared the stage when we both ran for President, but we were never opponents, only good friends and "faith brothers" seeking the same job. Neither of us got the job, but we both kept our souls! Mike has captured what has driven my wife, Karen, and I in our lives—that our ultimate worth is not money, fame, or a political office, but in the children we raise, the integrity we pass on to them, and the spiritual mark we leave on others. He has captured in this book what I hope more people will embrace—that a life "done well" is the best legacy we can leave.

—**Rick Santorum**, former US Senator, Candidate for President, and Best-Selling Author

I'm not just friends with the Huckabees, Mike and Janet are active members of our church, and I can attest that this is not just a book—it's their lifestyle to plan for the future by keeping spiritual things front and center. I hope you'll use this book for your own personal improvement, but perhaps use it for a small group study. And live your life to be DONE WELL!

—**Steve Vaggalis**, Lead Pastor of Destiny Worship Center, Destin, FL

I work every day to change the grips of poverty and hopelessness, and I realize that good intentions can't substitute godly people living for something eternal. My friend Mike Huckabee lays out a powerful yet practical path to being ready to finish well in this life to be ready for the next one.

—**Star Parker**, Nationally Syndicated Columnist, President of UrbanCure, and Social Policy Ponsultant

I've argued numerous cases before the US Supreme Court, but one day we will all stand before the Supreme Judge whose rulings are just and eternal. In his latest book, my longtime friend Mike Huckabee scrapes away all the temporal and shallow goals people strive for to remind us that it's the LAST thing that is the *most* important thing. I know you'll enjoy his straight to the heart style and his straight to the heart message to be ready, not just for the next day of your life, but the LAST day of your life!

—**Mat Staver**, Founder and Chairman of Liberty Counsel, Former Dean of Liberty University Law School

Rare, Medium or Done Well is not a cookbook, but it does thoughtfully examine life's daily menu of choices that ultimately add up to make us the people we are. Insightful, uplifting, and hopeful, Mike Huckabee has examined what lies ahead and nudges us to all live beyond this lifetime. How do you do that? It's easy . . . if you know where to start.

—**Steve Doocy**, Host of Fox and Friends

Mike Huckabee worked for me as a young man and made a profound, positive impact. Now, as a great spokesman and statesman for the nation, Mike upholds the principles essential to faith, family, and freedom. His powerful book reveals the secrets of his success while demonstrating the potential for everyone to succeed. Above all, it maps the road to success and greatness for future generations of Americans.

—**James Robison**, Founder and President of
LIFE Outreach International, Fort Worth, Texas

Many of us know Governor Mike Huckabee for his impressive resume as a pastor, politician, author, and commentator—but as he shares in his latest book, these aren't the achievements he cherishes most. Instead, Governor Huckabee urges readers to consider what truly matters: faith, family, and generous service to others. This volume is sure to inspire many folks to take an honest look at what makes for a life "done well."

—**Jim Daly**, President of Focus on the Family

Making money, being famous, or having power possibly only lasts a lifetime, but there is a life lived that outlasts our time on earth and Mike Huckabee's message is an urgent reminder for all of us.

—**Michael Youssef**, Host of the global ministry
Leading The Way with Dr. Michael Youssef

If you could combine the wisdom of Mother Teresa, Vince Lombardi, and Tony Robinson into one book, the title would be *Rare, Medium or Done Well: Make the Most of Your Life* by Mike Huckabee. He has hit it out of the ballpark with this offering.

—**Michael Evans**, #1 *New York Times* Best-Selling Author

Mike Huckabee and I have been friends for over 30 years and I've watched his life from being a pastor, denominational leader, political candidate, and governor. Mike Huckabee is a real friend and his life is reflected in this outstanding book. His faithfulness and consistency throughout his life is a living message that helps prepare you for your greatest days in the future. He shares with you how to live, how to face the end of your life in this world, and then challenges you to leave a legacy. This book is a game changer for your future.

—**Dr. Ronnie Floyd**, Senior Pastor of Cross Church, Arkansas

Governor Mike Huckabee has been my friend since seminary days in the late 70's. Watching him keep the faith throughout his fascinating journey and unrivaled success as a pastor, politician, and parent has been an encouragement to all who have known him up close. As I read his new book, *Rare, Medium or Done Well: Make the Most of Your Life*, I realized that the classmate whom I first met over coffee 41 years ago still carries the same values and commitments that I so admired then. You can see Mike Huckabee in every word of this book, for he's sharing insights from the life he lived. *Rare, Medium or Done Well* deals candidly with all the root issues that are confronting our beloved nation, offering real and tangible biblical solutions that work. He makes it clear that everyone has a role to play in recovering our nation. I highly recommend this book. I was enriched by reading it.

—**Dr. Rick Scarborough**, Founder of Vision America
and Skyline Pastor, Washington, D.C.

We face opposition every day that convinces us that our lives and the decisions we make don't matter or have consequences. Governor Huckabee refutes that claim with picture-perfect clarity in *Rare, Medium or Done Well*. This book is a guide to realigning your priorities. It's a splash of encouraging water to the discouraged face!

—**Josh Turner**, multiple GRAMMY, CMA,
and ACM nominated country music artist,
one of youngest members of Grand Ole Opry

Many people only know Mike Huckabee as a political figure, but what really makes him tick is his faith and his latest book explores whether people are unprepared (Rare), mediocre (Medium), or ready for life's final chapter (Done Well). This is a great small group study book or just for personal reflection and edification.

—**Dr. Jim Garlow**, Senior Pastor of Skyline Church, San Diego, CA

In *Rare, Medium or Done Well* Mike Huckabee has not just written a great book *about* living a life of purpose, he *lives* it! If you are looking for a book that will challenge and equip you to live a life that matters, then you've found it. I love this book and believe our country needs its message today as never before.

—**Dr. Dennis Rainey**, Cofounder of FamilyLife
and Host of FamilyLife Today

My friend Mike Huckabee knows that the ultimate judgement of our lives won't be by the media or voters, but the God of creation. In this very winsome book, Huckabee artfully and, at times, humorously leads the reader toward a life DONE WELL. We all need this reminder of what matters most is what lasts forever. You will enjoy and be blessed by this message!

—**Robert Jeffress**, Sr. Pastor, First Baptist Church, Dallas, TX

I know and love Mike Huckabee for many reasons, but one of them is that he seems perpetually full of joy. In *Rare, Medium or Done Well: Make the Most of Your Life* you find out why. He's put the long term—including the eternal—over the day to day. So living well is not living rich, but living to be prepared for what people say about us when we're gone. Now that is called forward thinking! And did I mention it's fun to read? As a writer myself, I take that seriously!

—**Eric Metaxas**, *New York Times* Best-Selling Author of *Martin Luther*,
Nationally Syndicated Radio Host

Rare, Medium *or* Done Well

MAKE THE MOST OF YOUR LIFE

Mike Huckabee

WORTHY®
PUBLISHING

Published by Worthy Books, an imprint of Worthy Publishing Group, a division of Worthy Media, Inc., One Franklin Park, 6100 Tower Circle, Suite 210, Franklin, TN 37067.

WORTHY is a registered trademark of Worthy Media, Inc.

HELPING PEOPLE EXPERIENCE THE HEART OF GOD

eBook available wherever digital books are sold.

Cataloging-in-Publication Data is on file with the Library of Congress.

For foreign and subsidiary rights, contact rights@worthypublishing.com

Published in association with Frank Breeden of Premiere Authors | Shaker Heights, OH

ISBN: 978-1-68397-302-7 (Jacketed Hardcover)
ISBN: 978-1-68397-316-4 (TBN Special Edition)

Originally published as *Living Beyond Your Lifetime* © 2000 by Mike Huckabee

Cover Design: Matt Smartt, Smartt Guys Design
Cover Image: David Dobson, https://daviddobsonphoto.com/
Interior Design and Typesetting: Bart Dawson

Printed in the United States of America
18 19 20 21 22 LBM 8 7 6 5 4 3 2 1

This book is dedicated first to the memory of my parents, who gave me a legacy of believing that character and integrity are more valuable than wealth and that what we possess is less important than what kind of people we are.

Dorsey W. Huckabee, 1923–1996
Mae Elder Huckabee, 1925–1999

I further dedicate this book to my children and my grandchildren. When I wrote the original edition of this book, my children weren't married and there were no grandchildren. Now I have six grandkids who bring me more joy than I ever imagined. They also bring me anxiety about the world they will inherit, and I genuinely hope I will leave them a legacy that will help them be all God created them to be.

CONTENTS

Part Three | A LEGACY LIVED

Part Four | A LEGACY LOVED

Foreword

FORMER GOVERNOR MIKE HUCKABEE, a true leader, writes about lasting legacies. This book effectively makes the point that service to others and thinking of generations to come is a lot of what life is all about.

There can be no definition of a successful life that does not include service to others, and Former Governor Huckabee in *Rare, Medium, or Done Well* drives home that point.

—George H. W. Bush
Former President of the United States

Author's Note

THIS PROJECT WAS a therapeutic experience for me, especially since my mother's death occurred between the time I started the first edition of this book and the time I finished it.

When I completed the first version of this manuscript, I felt it was about my own pilgrimage of accepting the harsh reality that, with the death of both my parents, there was no longer anyone in my bloodline upstream from me. I needed to work through those deeply held feelings.

This book is straightforward and candid. I haven't tried to be a writer as much a friend and even encourager to those who will read it. I hope you feel as if we are having a conversation over a cup of coffee or iced tea on a porch overlooking some water.

In the following chapters, I hope you'll be challenged to think about living a life that is done well. This is the kind of life that is neither unprepared for the future (rare) nor rising to the highest level of mediocrity (medium). Instead, a life done well has lasting effects that will be felt long after you leave this earth by those who wouldn't be the same if the seeds of your faith and faithfulness had not been planted.

partying and using drugs. Worse, he began hanging out with the local gangs his father had been trying to shield him from.

Thankfully, the University of Florida gave him a football scholarship and a fresh start. Aaron had a standout career at Florida, helping the Gators win the 2009 BCS National Championship and being recognized as a first-team All-American. With his stardom on the rise, he decided to forgo his senior season and enter the NFL Draft.

But several off-field incidents in Florida revealed that Aaron was making the same kinds of poor choices he had made in high school. He failed multiple drug tests and was charged with possession of marijuana. One night he got into a drunken fight with a restaurant employee after refusing to pay his bill, and a few months later, he and four other University of Florida players were questioned about a shooting.

Because of these and other issues, Aaron fell to the fourth round of the 2010 NFL Draft. He was signed by the New England Patriots, starting the 2010 season as the youngest player on any active roster in the NFL. He appeared to embrace this new start, playing three successful seasons with the Patriots and even helping lead the team to Super Bowl XLVI. Aaron was finally on his way to achieving his fairy-tale ending of fame, fortune, and Super Bowl titles.

Yet living so close to his hometown, Aaron was unable to resist going back to the gang life. Just ten months after he signed a $40 million contract with the Patriots in 2012, Aaron was charged with the murder of a friend, Odin Lloyd. After Aaron's arrest, the Patriots released Hernandez from his contract. In 2015, Aaron Hernandez was convicted of first-degree murder and sentenced to life in prison without the possibility of parole. He was later accused in two other cases, one for double murder and attempted murder and one for witness intimidation.

By 2017, Aaron's success story was over. His money and career were gone. His endorsement deals were cancelled, his likeness was erased from popular video games, his award-winning photo was taken out of the Pro Football Hall of Fame, and his memorabilia and merchandise were removed from the University of Florida and NFL pro shops. He had few supporters or friends. As one commentator put it, "He was no longer Aaron Hernandez the Super Bowl tight end, the star of Boston's nightclubs or even the celebrity defendant. He was just a 27-year-old convicted killer doomed to live his life in a prison cell."[1]

In the early morning hours of April 19, 2017, on the same day his Patriots teammates were scheduled to celebrate another Super Bowl victory at the White House, Aaron Hernandez's body was discovered tied with a bedsheet to his prison cell in Shirley, Massachusetts. His death was ruled a suicide.

Aaron Hernandez's life is a stark reminder that some life stories, no matter how promising, just don't end "happily ever after." At such times, it becomes more important than ever to begin assessing the difference between the immediate and the ultimate. What we do and how we live really do matter.

When we act on our passions of the moment and succumb to the feelings of "right now" without regard for the impact these actions will have, we have committed a grievous sin—letting our *lifestyle* ruin our *lifetime*.

Life Is Not a Dress Rehearsal

I once was visiting in an office and noticed a sign that proclaimed, "Enjoy life. This is not a dress rehearsal." That simple message stuck with me and still does.

How painfully true that is. Life is not a dress rehearsal. This is the real thing. We make choices that have consequences for a lifetime.

This book seeks to challenge our culture's perspective of "If it feels good, do it." For decades, our nation has been focused on personal pleasure. Baby boomers were known as the "Me" generation. Today's generation has been dubbed "iGen," with young people so fixated on self and selfies that even our gadgets start with *I*. Modern advertising bombards us with the message that life is all about me; it is all about now.

> When we act on our passions of the moment and succumb to the feelings of "right now" without regard for the impact these actions will have, we have committed a grievous sin— letting our *lifestyle* ruin our *lifetime*.

Such messages may sell products and services, but they will cause us to sell our souls if we follow this philosophy to its logical conclusion.

At some point in life, we will all experience events that shake up our everyday routine, much like the agitator in the washing machine shakes loose the grime in our clothes. Such experiences are neither desired nor enjoyed. But they are necessary to force us to focus on the frailty of life and the certainty of death. They also force us to begin asking what really matters and why.

It is a safe bet that one hundred years from today, most of us will have passed from this life. We have no way of knowing if we have already celebrated our last birthday or observed our final Christmas. We will be challenged from time to time to ask whether in the final analysis our lives really mattered and, if so, in what way and for whom. If we live and then die, and that is all there is, then it may not matter a great deal what we do or how well we do it. But if we believe there is even a remote possibility that our actions have lasting implications beyond our lifetime, this should cause us to think differently, live differently, and leave a different kind of legacy.

Living Beyond Your Lifetime

Without apology, I believe the spiritual side of our lives really does matter. To believe otherwise is, in essence, to define humans as little more than animated protoplasm hopelessly going about our routines for no particular purpose. I prefer to believe that, as spiritual beings, there is more to us than flesh and blood. If we do possess a soul capable of living beyond our lifetimes, then the seeds we plant in this life will yield fruit forever. If you believe those things, the ultimate becomes more important than the immediate.

When we decide to live beyond our lifetime, our responsibilities to the next generation will outweigh our roles in our current jobs. More important than the money we are paid for our work is what we will become as a result of our work. Our character will become more critical than the careers we follow.

For all of us, life began "once upon a time." Unlike the fairy tales, however, it is up to you to make the choices that determine whether the last line of your life story will read, "And they lived happily ever after."

QUESTIONS FOR REFLECTION AND DISCUSSION

1. What experiences have you had that made you realize life is not always like a fairy tale—that not everyone ends up living "happily ever after"?

2. What evidence do you see that our culture promotes the idea, "If it feels good, do it"?

3. In your opinion, what are some of the characteristics of a life that really matters? What are some of the characteristics of a life that counts for nothing?

4. What do you think the author means by this statement: "As spiritual beings, there is more to us than flesh and blood"?

5. Do you believe that what we do and how we live really matters? Why or why not?

2

POTATO SALAD TIME

I HAD NEVER FELT SO ALONE IN MY LIFE.

I stood in a well-kept cemetery just off highway US 67 in Hope, Arkansas. I stared at the cold stone marker on which the names of my parents were etched, along with the dates of their births and the dates of their deaths.

It was rare for me to be alone. I had asked the governor's security detail from the Arkansas State Police to give me some space. My mother had died on the last day of September 1999. For the first time since I showed up on this planet, my only family links, other than my sister and my wife, were my descendants. When my mother drew her last breath, I became the oldest living link my children had in their bloodlines on my side of the family.

The depth of my grief was not so much over the circumstances of my mother's death. Since a brain aneurysm and series of strokes in early 1992, her health had declined steadily. In her last days, it was no longer merciful to pray for continued existence as she was experiencing it. I was comforted by my unwavering faith that there was in fact a God in whose arms she would fall. I knew death was not the worst thing that could happen to her. Continuing in her state would, in fact, have been worse.

It wasn't so much that she had died as it was the fact that her death had closed the book on an entire generation. Her passing had taken away my last link to the past and forever physically separated me from the one in whose womb I was formed.

It would have been easier if I could have wept bitterly. God has a wonderful way of washing away our grief with a cleansing shower of tears. But some pain is far too intense to be expressed with the same emotions we once used for a scraped knee, a sad movie, or a loss in a championship basketball game. In that moment, I understood better Romans 8:26: "The Spirit also helps in our weaknesses. For we do not know what we should pray for as we ought, but the Spirit Himself makes intercession for us with groanings which cannot be uttered" (NKJV). The phrase "groanings which cannot be uttered" became more meaningful as I sought in the depth of my soul to find a vehicle of expression for my grief.

None of us gets to choose how we come into this world. We can't choose our parents, our hometown, or the physician who ushers us into this life. Unless we end our lives by our own hands, neither do we choose the circumstances or date of our deaths.

Even though we don't choose how we start life or how we end it, we most certainly choose how we live. It is how we live that may determine how people feel as they stand staring at our names chiseled into the gravestones. It is how we live that will affect generations to come and countless people whose names we don't even know.

In the South, there's a time-honored tradition that friends of the deceased bring more food to the grieving family than can ever be eaten. Obesity among Southerners may in fact be tied to the number of funerals we are part of. After a loved one dies, there will soon be a parade of people, a pastor's visit, lots of hugs, and, without fail, large bowls of potato salad. The potato salad is such a Southern fixture during the period of grief that some refer to it as "potato salad time."

> Even though we don't choose how we start life or how we end it, we most certainly choose how we live.

"Potato salad time" is a good time to do some serious reflection about what really matters. No matter how busy we are, it's often in the presence of the potato salad that we are brought to a halt and reminded of how temporary this life is. Consuming large quantities of potato salad may not be good for your health, but being consumed by overwhelming doses of reality can be helpful.

The Value of a Life That Matters

You don't have to leave behind millions of dollars to have lived a life that mattered. The size of your tombstone doesn't indicate the size of your life. I sometimes take casual walks through cemeteries and read the tombstones. You can learn a lot by reading information on tombstones about those whose voices are stilled but whose legacies live on. Most of their names never made the headlines. More died poor than rich in terms of money accumulated. But many of

or even a young adult. But Janet and I have realized that having more is really the opportunity to give more, and we have delighted in giving more to our church than we used to dream of earning, or simply being able to leave a tip for a server that was more than the meal cost just to be a blessing to someone who was working hard and probably needed an unexpected boost for that day. We have discovered that the value of a life done well cannot be measured in bank accounts or stock portfolios. One of the simple joys of a life done well is giving generously and freely to others.

The Legacy of a Life That Matters

I remember vividly the first time I stood at the Tomb of the Unknown Soldier at Arlington National Cemetery in Virginia. The soldier known only to God left not so much as his name, yet he is honored twenty-four hours a day, seven days a week. He represents the high cost of our American freedom. It's inconceivable to me that any American could stand at that place and not feel a sense of gratitude and pride.

> One of the simple joys of a life done well is giving generously and freely to others.

I also have visited the great pyramids of Egypt twice and marveled at the elaborate tombs of the ancient Egyptian pharaohs. While I was impressed with the architecture and innovation of the magnificent pyramids, I was struck with the thought that so much effort was made for the dead. You can't help but wonder if the effort might have been more productive had it been made for the living.

I've also visited the cemetery near Mount Zion in Jerusalem and stood at the grave of Oskar Schindler, who was immortalized in Steven Spielberg's Oscar-winning film *Schindler's List*. Oskar Schindler failed at marriage and at business. But he left a legacy because, when he had the opportunity, he acted to save the lives of others. Entire generations of Jewish families owe their existence to his courage and sacrifice.

Perhaps the most vivid memories come from my many trips to Jerusalem and the two places vying for designation as the likely burial spot of Jesus Christ. The one thing the tombs have in common is that they are both empty. The thousands of visitors who flock to these sites each day to see that "He has risen! He is not here" (Mark 16:6) remind us of the most important legacy of all. That's the fact that this life, though important, is not the only one we live for. When our time on this earth is over, we will, by faith, share the legacy of our Lord as we enter into eternal life in heaven with him.

The choices we make in this life really matter. The seeds we plant during our lives will bear fruit through those who live beyond us and our "potato salad time."

QUESTIONS FOR REFLECTION AND DISCUSSION

1. What's the difference between owning things and being owned by things?

2. What kind of legacy have people like Oskar Schindler left the world?

3. What legacy have your parents left you?

4. What type of legacy are you working to leave for others?

5. Which do you think is more important: a material legacy or a spiritual legacy? Why?

THE CULTURE
OF THE MOMENT

DICK MORRIS SAT ON THE EDGE OF THE BED in the small, crowded room on the sixth floor of the Camelot Hotel in downtown Little Rock. It was 8:30 p.m. on July 29, 1993, and the polls had been closed for less than an hour after a special election for the office of lieutenant governor. This was the only item on the ballot in Arkansas that day.

Ordinarily, an election for lieutenant governor would draw little media attention. But this race was different. The office was vacant because Arkansas's former governor, Bill Clinton, had been sworn in as president, and the lieutenant governor, Jim Guy Tucker, had moved up to governor.

The vacancy for lieutenant governor was in the political spotlight during the summer of 1993. The race had become much more than a contest for the office itself. It was the first major election in Arkansas following Clinton's move to the White House. Up to that point in 1993, Republicans had put together a clean sweep of major elections across America. Later that year, governor's races in New Jersey and Virginia would be claimed by the GOP.

On this hot and humid day, political eyes nationwide were focused on Arkansas to see what would happen in the new president's backyard. Morris was no stranger to Arkansas political races or to conducting political polls to determine how those races were going. He had worked for Clinton in every one of the president's political races except his unsuccessful 1974 race for Congress and his unsuccessful 1980 race for governor.

Only a handful of results came in during the first hour after the polls closed at 7:30 p.m. As each new total was posted, Morris would scratch furiously on a yellow legal pad and then enter the figures in a pocket calculator. Just past 8:30 p.m., with fewer than 15 percent of the precincts having reported, Morris turned to me and, in a matter-of-fact tone of voice, said, "Congratulations, you're going to be elected lieutenant governor with 51 percent of the vote."

It would be another ninety minutes before the rest of the ballots were counted and the results were clear enough for my opponent to concede and for me to walk on the stage and face a cheering crowd of supporters. I declared victory with 51 percent of the vote. How could he possibly have known the outcome so early with so little information?

That night, I recognized the power of scientific polling to recognize trends, attitudes, and movements of public opinion. In today's politics, having a competent pollster can be expensive, but not nearly as expensive as not having the information the pollster can generate. Good information ensures that the right campaign decisions are made. One of the valuable lessons I learned that night was that if you only have a small budget, spend enough of it to get accurate research. Spending what little money you have on a message that hasn't been carefully tested is not called "saving money"; it's called "losing the election."

During subsequent campaigns, I came to appreciate even more the value of public opinion research. Polling is much like using a thermometer. A thermometer can give an accurate measurement of what the temperature is at a given moment. What a thermometer cannot do, however, is adjust the temperature and make it what it should be. Similarly, polling can tell you where things are at a given moment, but it cannot make any needed changes.

> Our culture needs people whose lives are built upon clear, carefully considered principles.

It is important for a political candidate to know what the public believes. But for a candidate to express a belief only because it reflects current public sentiment is not what a republican form of government is about. Our culture needs people whose lives are built upon clear, carefully considered principles. Too many of our leaders today are making decisions based only on what people claim to want rather than what is truly right or wrong.

Principles Worth Living By

As a teenager in my hometown of Hope, Arkansas, I often heard my pastor say, "If you don't stand for something, you will fall for

4

THE POLITICS
OF PERSONAL
DESTRUCTION

PRESIDENT CLINTON COINED THE PHRASE "politics of personal destruction" during the Whitewater scandal and the subsequent impeachment process. Although he admitted he had lied to a grand jury, the president managed to avoid ouster from office. He did so by appealing to Americans' growing distaste for a political system in which candidates are portrayed as bad people rather than a system in which competing ideas are debated.

Unfortunately, the days since President Clinton have seen anything *but* a more civil political environment. In today's era of Twitter and "fake news," political and policy debates have largely been replaced with weaponized information and inference—or even downright assertion that a candidate or officeholder is guilty of criminal activity, most often by anonymous sources. These personal attacks are taking place on both sides of the political spectrum. Yet the foundation of our criminal justice system is that we are innocent until proven guilty beyond a reasonable doubt and that we are entitled to face our accusers. This is not just a hallmark of our American system, but it's one of the most significant things that distinguishes our nation from the rest of the world.

These days, accusations—even from unnamed and anonymous sources—are tantamount to guilt, and the accused is expected to refute phantom charges with concrete evidence. This is a substantial reason that many well-qualified and honorable people choose to stay far away from elective office or appointment to public service. They know that when one side doesn't win the election, its members will try to destroy the winning side through nonstop, and often untrue, accusations and allegations.

Elective politics is not the only realm in which there is overt and intentional character assassination. We see similar actions in the politics of the business office or even the politics of the church. It also can be true of marriage and the family. Many people decide that it is better to divorce their partners than to work to resolve conflict.

Even by the standards of Jesus, it is not wrong to have enemies. Jesus certainly had enemies! We can't keep people from hating us, but it is wrong for us to hate them. As we go through life, most of us will encounter people who are considered enemies. Someone once wisely said that we should love our enemies because they are the only ones who will always tell us the truth.

Jesus told his disciples, "You have heard that it was said, 'Love your neighbor and hate your enemy.' But I tell you, love your enemies and pray for those who persecute you, that you may be children of your Father in heaven" (Matthew 5:43–45). It is easy to love our friends. But loving our enemies requires an extraordinary touch of grace and a true understanding of what love means. Loving our enemies does not mean giving in to their demands or compromising our values. None of us has the capacity to control the actions of others. But we are responsible for our reactions to the behavior of others.

One of the most misunderstood admonitions of the Bible is the instruction on dealing with bad behavior that is directed toward us. The ancient code of retaliation known as "an eye for an eye" (Exodus 21:24) is actually a marked improvement over the more barbaric attitude, "Cut out my eye, and I will cut off your head."

> None of us has the capacity to control the actions of others. But we are responsible for our reactions to the behavior of others.

Most of our hearts are ruled more by a sense of revenge than a sense of justice. Revenge is a drive that is natural to us. We want more than just getting even. In Matthew 5:39–42, Jesus cited three examples of unfair actions that we might encounter. If we are struck on the right cheek, then we are to turn the other cheek. If someone sues us for our shirt, then we are admonished to give it up voluntarily along with our coat. And if we are forced to do a duty that we don't want to do, then we are encouraged to go the second mile— to do more than required.

In the ancient culture in which Jesus lived, a strike on the right cheek was an insulting blow to a person's dignity and pride. A person's coat represented his or her possessions, which were necessary for covering and warmth. And under Roman law, it was a person's duty to carry a soldier's equipment for up to one mile.

Jesus set new standards by telling us we should never be content to do only what is expected of us. We should go to the next level by living and giving beyond our obligations and expectations. The way to win over an enemy is not to conquer but to serve. When we go beyond the expected duties and responsibilities, we demonstrate excellence, leadership, and accomplishment: the higher qualities of a life done well.

The Danger of Denouncing Competitors

Getting ahead today often means disabling others so they are unable to complete the race. But such an approach does not represent getting ahead at all. There is no honor in such a victory—only shame. When the associates and ex-husband of former Olympic skater Tonya Harding were accused of attacking competitor Nancy Kerrigan, the world was repulsed. Without able and honorable competition, victory in any endeavor is meaningless. That incident was so notorious that over twenty years after it happened, Hollywood rolled out a movie about the incident called *I, Tonya*.

The restaurant that eliminates a competitor across the street by starting a whispering campaign about people getting food poisoning at that eatery might succeed for a time. Ultimately, though, quality and service of the surviving restaurant will decline without competition.

Loving others is not the same as performing according to the demands of others. We do not show love to an alcoholic by giving him what he craves—another drink. True love must draw the line and say no. Genuinely caring about another person does not necessarily mean doing what that person demands. By the same token, eliminating competition is not nearly as productive in the long term as besting the competition.

A basketball team that never plays a game but advances due to the forfeiture of other teams is not prepared to play its best. A politician who seeks to win an election by destroying the reputation of his opponents will eventually die by the sword he raised against others.

A life done well requires that we do not think in terms of getting rid of those who oppose us. Instead, we should overcome them with superior ideas and values. Race car drivers don't show their car is better by letting the air out of their opponents' tires; they prove it by racing their rivals side by side.

People whose principles are well grounded are not afraid of competition. Elijah challenged the prophets of Baal on Mount Carmel. After inviting them to call upon their god to consume a sacrifice on the altar, he called upon God to do the same (1 Kings 18:20–39). It is a big mistake for people of integrity and faith to believe that they will advance their cause by destroying the competition.

> The way to win over an enemy is not to conquer but to serve. When we go beyond the expected duties and responsibilities, we demonstrate excellence, leadership, and accomplishment: the higher qualities of a life done well.

been elected and held public office, and that is absolutely hard work! I have also been employed in radio and television and talked about the people who ran for and held public office—and frankly, it's the easiest job I've ever had, but amazingly, it pays much better than anything I've ever done. At least when I discuss politics and offer commentary, I do so from the perspective of having been in the arena. I have been often tempted when hearing TV personalities (even the ones I like and work with) speak with "authority" as to what an elected official should do, to say to them, "If you know so much as to how it should be done, then let's see *your* name on the ballot next election!"

My family has had to endure attacks I never would have imagined before running for office. Frivolous lawsuits instigated by political opponents who are unable to find real issues can create distractions from the tasks at hand. Some members of the media are willing not only to report baseless allegations but to repeat them over and over. I've even had so-called journalists initiate an ethics complaint and then report on it without disclosing that they had created it.

Although attacking opponents will sometimes work with voters, it will not work as we stand before God's judgment seat. He will judge each of us based on what he knows about us, not on what our critics have said about us.

QUESTIONS FOR REFLECTION AND DISCUSSION

1. In this chapter, the author describes our nation's political climate as "the politics of personal destruction." Do you agree or disagree with this assessment? What evidence of this "personal destruction" approach have you observed in recent political campaigns?

2. Do you agree or disagree with this statement: "Genuinely caring about another person does not necessarily mean doing what that person demands"? Explain your answer.

3. In what ways does God's judgment of us differ from the human judgments that most of us have to endure?

4. In your opinion, why did Jesus exhort us to love our enemies?

5. Describe the ancient code of retaliation known as "an eye for an eye." Do you think that is an effective form of justice? Why or why not?

5

FAMILIES
IN FREE FALL

THE YOUNG MINISTER STOOD before a large congregation, performing the first wedding ceremony of his career. Not even the bride was as nervous as the newly ordained pastor. He feared butchering a high-dollar wedding involving one of the church's most influential families.

Soon, his anxiety turned to terror. Having seated the audience, the pastor opened his Bible, only to realize he had forgotten to place his notes for the wedding ceremony in the pages. He thought he could recite the ceremony by memory, but to calm himself he decided to begin by quoting some Scripture.

Unfortunately, as he stood facing the bride and groom and hundreds of waiting guests, the Scripture that came to his mind and out of his mouth was, "Father, forgive them, for they know not what they do."

The young minister was probably more right than wrong in his assessment of the situation before him. Our culture is failing in its understanding of the proper role of marriage. A substantial number of marriages performed in the United States will end in divorce. And the likelihood of divorce increases sharply in second and third marriages.

Back in the 1990s, my home state of Arkansas had one of the highest divorce rates in the nation.[1] Fortunately, these numbers have changed somewhat. I challenged the people in my state to reduce the divorce rate by half during the next decade by declaring a state of marital emergency. We encouraged pastors in each city to adopt community marriage policies in which couples are required to have premarital counseling.

Why does it matter? While there are many wonderful exceptions for which we can be grateful, the overwhelming statistical evidence points out that divorce dramatically increases the likelihood of poverty. Children growing up without the benefit of two parents are more likely to get involved in drugs, alcohol, premarital sex, juvenile delinquency, and academic failure. The cost to society for failed marriages is too high to calculate. In most instances, only the lawyers come out winners.

One of the reasons so many marriages fail is that couples have accepted the myth that the purpose of marriage is to be happy. If a couple's expectations for a marriage arise from a sentimental love story filled with constant excitement, adventure, and romance, then they are headed for disappointment. The reality is that marriage is a cultural collision. Two independent individuals who have lived under different rules, habits, and lifestyles suddenly join together in a relationship designed to be a lifelong laboratory of learning how to love.

What Is the Goal of Marriage?

Years ago, I told a young couple during premarital counseling that God's primary goal for their marriage was not necessarily for them to be happy. The groom interrupted and said, "Well, that is good to hear. Apparently, we are succeeding."

If the goal of marriage is not to be happy, then what is it?

The word *happiness* is derived from "happenstance," suggesting a pleasure that is derived from external conditions that are subject to change. According to this definition, happiness is based on how we feel and what kinds of conditions surround us—whether we have good health, plenty of money, friends who support us, and an absence of conflict, illness, and unexpected calamity.

Few people experience a life of consistent pleasure. Most of us live in an imperfect world. The toast is burned. Our car battery is dead. The traffic on the way to work is horrible. Other drivers are rude. The boss is mean. We get notice of an IRS audit. The dog chews up our favorite shoes. The long-anticipated football game is interrupted by an outage of the cable system.

Since God performed the first wedding, and since he authored life and the instructions on how to live it, we need to discover exactly what his instructions are for marriage before we seek to live it.

of self-love." To understand how we are to love others, we need to look not in the mirror but toward heaven. We are to discern how God loves us.

God does not love us because we are lovable. He does not love us because we meet certain conditions—such as giving a specific amount to charity, attending church, or even being polite. He loves us because it is his nature and his choice to love us. He loves us without regard for whether we are worthy, will return his love, or even acknowledge his existence.

No matter how good we are, God can love us no more than he already does. And no matter how bad we are, God can love us no less than he already does. God's love for us is prompted by nothing we do. It comes from his own character.

Unlike God, we do not have a natural aptitude for this kind of sacrificial, selfless love. We are born with the desire to put ourselves first. Human nature drives us to make sure our own needs are met. Sin is spelled with a big *I* in the middle.

Even when we pretend to be humble, there are those moments in which our true nature bursts forth. Have you been part of a group photograph recently? When you had a chance to look at it, perhaps tagged in someone's post on social media, whose image did you glance at first? Did you judge how good the photo was based on how you looked?

When marriage is based on how we feel, we are headed for disaster. Marriage should be based not on our emotions but on our devotion and what we choose to do in seeking the best for our partners. Marriages fail for the same reason that people fail. They are overwhelmed with selfishness. One of the great promises of the

Bible is that God will never leave us or forsake us (Hebrews 13:5). Yet far too many marriages are based on the premise that "If you don't perform up to my expectations, then I will leave you and forsake you."

None of us stands at the marriage altar and expects our marriage to fail. Divorce is the unnatural conclusion to a relationship that started with wonderful expectations and ended with deep hurt and shattered hopes. But no amount of prayer or patience can hold a marriage together when one of the partners is determined to destroy it.

> A marriage in which the two partners don't actually need each other is a marriage that has already failed.

Every married couple should understand that marriage was designed to last a lifetime. Marriage should teach us how to love. Marriage is more than a temporary lifestyle in which we use another person in order to meet our own needs. The basis for a successful marriage is not that two people learn to be independent. Rather, they choose to relinquish their independence for the purpose of building a relationship of interdependence. A marriage in which the two partners don't actually need each other is a marriage that has already failed.

It is the nature of a husband to want to be wanted. A man is motivated if he believes his wife truly needs and wants him. A wife must have similar feelings about her husband. When a couple does not share a mutual need for each other, they are headed toward disaster.

One of the tragedies of a failed marriage is that it sends the message to children that marriage is temporary rather than forever. It retailer publish what they deemed a "catalog" with occasional references to their merchandise mixed with stories of a pedophile whose job as a department store Santa Claus gave him the opportunity to delight in little girls bouncing on his lap.

There also were stories of a pornographic movie star, complete with nude photos of her and her graphic descriptions of a promiscuous sex life. There was frontal nudity throughout the catalog. Most of the females captured in the nude appeared to be young teenagers, often in the embrace of males who looked to be in their thirties.

The company asserted that all the women photographed were older than eighteen. In comparison to some pornographic magazines on the newsstand, this catalog could indeed be considered tame. But it was repulsive that such a publication was being used to market trendy clothing to teenagers. One television commentator discussing the resulting publicity furor remarked how ironic it was for a company to try to sell clothing by picturing people who were not wearing any.

The company defended its publication, saying that it came in a plastic wrap with a warning sticker. Obviously, they said, it was intended for adults. If that defense were valid, then cigarette smoking would have ended in this country three decades ago based on the warning labels printed on each pack.

I do not call for our government to determine what people can or can't believe or what they can or can't see. As governor, I had no power to order such marketing ploys off the shelves. However, my role as a parent caused me to explain to my daughter why I would no longer spend my money to buy clothing for her at that store.

A Tragic Legacy of Lust

If we want our lives to be done well, then we need to avoid confusing lust with love. There is something tragic about a culture that loses the capacity to express sacrificial love. In our nation, we are increasingly abandoning that idea in exchange for ego-centered love that uses other people as vehicles for our personal satisfaction.

Defenders of pornography point to the US Constitution. Indeed, the First Amendment protects material that is merely offensive. But repeated US Supreme Court decisions have affirmed that obscenity is not protected free speech. Even if the Constitution did allow for child pornography, bestiality, and female mutilation, for people of faith there is a document that is more binding than the Constitution and clearer in its understanding of right and wrong.

> If we want our lives to be done well, then we need to avoid confusing lust with love.

In today's sensuality-saturated culture, we are trading a legacy of love for a legacy of lust in at least five ways.

Attack Against Morality

It might surprise you to know that I'm not nearly the prude my critics portray me to be. Nudity in art and the movies is not automatically offensive to me. I don't use profanity or tolerate it in my workplaces, but I recognize it is a part of our culture and accept it as part of the language we must live with. It is not the presence of such things that are offensive. It is the context in which they are presented that moves them from expression to excess. Too often, nudity and profanity are used so a weak idea can receive strong attention.

Society's view of sensuality has changed dramatically since Hugh Hefner came out with the first edition of *Playboy* magazine. Who would have thought that a generation later what was then a scandalous adult magazine would be milder than a catalog published by a retailer trying to attract business from teenagers?

As we pass the generational torch, perhaps we should ask if we are better off as a nation because of these changes. Are families stronger? Are schools safer? Are incest, rape, and child molestation less prevalent today? Do our children have more respect for teachers, God, and government? Are people more content with themselves and their marriages?

If we are a better nation, then why do drug dogs patrol our school campuses? Why do we find it necessary to build rape crisis centers? Why must our police officers wear bulletproof vests as part of their standard equipment? Why is our country in need of more psychiatric hospitals than ever before?

No one would suggest that obscene materials are the sole cause of the deterioration of our morals. A strong argument can be made that private morals are private and not the domain of government. But a stronger argument can be made that the public has the right to determine what is in the best interest of all citizens.

We regulate liquor sales and used car dealers. We make sure the kitchens in restaurants are clean. Even if we don't eat in a certain restaurant, our taxes help pay to have it inspected. When sex crimes are committed, our tax dollars pay the court costs, the prison costs, the social service costs. The issue moves from private morality to public morality.

Citizens do, in fact, have the right to determine what they consider appropriate as a society. It has become a cliché to shout, "You can't legislate morality!" But this is a contradictory statement. All legislation determines the morality of an issue. It would be correct to say that you cannot legislate behavior. But every law sets a moral standard for society.

Speeding laws determine what is wrong when it comes to how fast you drive. Laws prohibiting murder define the morality of killing. We can't force people to believe the same things we do, but self-governing people do have the right to place boundaries on what can be bought and sold, whether it is heroin, a prostitute's body, or videos that depict adults having sex with children.

Attack Against the Mind

University studies from the United States and Canada confirm that pornography is addictive and progressive. Most people move from mild to more bizarre forms of pornography over time. In the more extreme cases, movies about sex with animals and with children are marketed to those who no longer are titillated by an airbrushed photo of a topless twenty-year-old.

The day before his execution for multiple murders, rapes, and acts of sexual torture against women and children, Ted Bundy confessed that the pornography he saw as a child fed his obsession for more

All legislation determines the morality of an issue. It would be correct to say that you cannot legislate behavior. But every law sets a moral standard for society.

until he progressed to a state of total depravity. Counselors can attest to the fact that there are indeed "pornoholics." Unlike those who sneak an occasional peek at sexually explicit material, these people are increasingly addicted to more explicit versions of smut. And with the rise of pornography on the Internet, they now have instant access to this denigrating content twenty-four hours a day, seven days a week.

Attack Against Marriage

A person who will gaze at an electronically enhanced photo of a model in a magazine or online will tend to view his spouse with increasing disrespect. The reality is that the flesh-and-blood spouse often contrasts sharply with the Photoshopped fantasy of the magazine page, video, or computer screen. The needs of many wives go unmet because their husbands are trying to meet their own needs through sexual encounters with photographs. These men seek to satisfy their sexual needs with photographs of women they don't know, while the wives they have promised to cherish are neglected.

And pornography is no longer primarily a man's problem. An increasing number of women today admit that they, too, struggle with porn. Recent studies have shown that more than 60 percent of women have viewed porn by age eighteen, and 1 in 5 women admit to habitually viewing Internet porn at least once a week.[1] It should come as no surprise, then, that with so many husbands and wives fantasizing over airbrushed images and impossible ideals, they are becoming increasingly dissatisfied with their real-life marriages.

Attack Against Motherhood

Sex for trade is an affront to the values we need in the mothers of America's children. Would anyone suggest it is a nurturing environment for a child to have a mother who sleeps with a different man every night? Do we want children growing up believing that a woman's value is based on her external beauty while denying the existence of inner beauty and character?

Attack Against Manhood

Sexually explicit materials perpetuate the myth that a real man treats women with savage selfishness. Pornography encourages a man to view his sexual partner as a plaything to be discarded when "it" no longer brings him pleasure. This furthers the lie that sex is primarily physical. We forget the spiritual and emotional dimensions that God intended us to experience when he created sex. The modern view of sex reduces a person's highest worth to a mere bodily function and forsakes the meaning of honor, character, and consideration for others.

I have yet to meet a man who wants his son to grow up and become a customer of prostitutes. I have never had a man say to me that his goal was for his son to become so addicted to porn that it keeps him from enjoying a lifetime with a decent family. I have yet to meet a man who dreams that his child will be a centerfold model or a porn star, with strange eyes leering lustfully at the image. It is inconceivable that any father would want his child to be the object of thousands of strangers who fantasize themselves in bed with him or her.

There is a point at which feminists and most conservatives agree: it is disgusting to treat people as objects and not respect their personhood. Every human being deserves to be treated with dignity and respect. An individual should never be considered as another person's property. I cannot imagine that any sane person would argue that we return to a system of slavery. But pornography does just that. It enslaves the viewer in a downward spiral of lust and seeks to make slaves of those who are the objects of lustful desire.

> There is a point at which feminists and most conservatives agree: it is disgusting to treat people as objects and not respect their personhood.

Why is it necessary to deal with this topic as we consider how to live a life done well? Let's hope it is because we have finally tired as a society of seeing the tears of those whose spouses have come to love the online videos or pages of a magazine more than their real-life partners. I hope we have grown tired of hearing five- and six-year-old children tell of being molested. I hope it is because we have tired of seeing the devastation of young people who are promised love but given lust by hormone-driven adolescents who are ready to toss aside one person they treated as a toy in pursuit of yet another.

What About Our Freedom?

Some of you reading this chapter may be protesting, "What about our freedom? Do we have the right to do as we please?" Yes, we are free, but as the famous saying goes, "Your right to swing your arms ends just where the other man's nose begins." In other words, our individual freedom has common-sense limits.

- We are free to drive, but the law restricts our speed, which direction we travel, and whether we wear seat belts.
- We are free to be filthy, but we are not free to walk into a hospital operating room in that condition.
- We are free to vote, but we are not free to vote on someone else's ballot or vote more than once.
- We are free to express an opinion, but we are not free to play a loudspeaker in a neighborhood at 2:00 a.m.
- We are free to worship, but we are not free to sit down in a busy intersection to pray, backing up traffic for miles.
- We are free to publish, but we are not free to libel others.
- We are free to assemble with others, but we are not free to plot the overthrow of our government.
- We are free to drink liquor, but we are not free to do it when we are ten years old or to get intoxicated in public.

A person is free to be "sexually liberated" and think slimy thoughts. A person is free to believe women and children are worthless objects to be used for another's pleasure. A person is free to let his or her mind be used as a toxic waste dump. But when a person takes an action that carries out those thoughts, his freedom ends.

The argument I have heard most often as it relates to sexually explicit materials is, "Where is the harm?" Perhaps it is better to ask, "Where is the good?"

If our society continues down the path of pornography, will we enhance the attitude of children about their sexuality? Will we better prepare our teenagers for marriage and parenthood? Will we teach our young people to live lives of integrity, value, and dignity?

If one child is victimized, if one woman is raped and forever traumatized, if one teenage girl is exploited and emotionally destroyed because of pornography—then this legacy of lust is not worth the risk.

> How we raise our children today when it comes to respecting themselves and others may determine the survival of our society.

Jesus is often depicted as mild-mannered. But throughout the Bible, we see that Jesus got angry over how people were treated, and he became livid when he saw people being exploited. There was nothing mild-mannered when he said, "It would be better for them to be thrown into the sea with a millstone tied around their neck than to cause one of these little ones to stumble" (Luke 17:2). How we raise our children today when it comes to respecting themselves and others may determine the survival of our society.

QUESTIONS FOR REFLECTION AND DISCUSSION

1. Do you agree or disagree with this statement: "You can't legislate morality"? Explain your answer.

2. What did you learn in this chapter about whether pornography is addictive? What is a "pornoholic"?

3. In what ways do pornography and illicit sexual relationships cheapen sex?

4. According to the author, what are some limitations to a person's individual freedoms? What other examples of common-sense limits of individual freedoms can you think of?

5. In your opinion, what can individual Christians and churches do to combat pornography and sexually explicit materials in our society?

Part Two

A LEGACY LEARNED

7

PARENTS
DO MATTER

THE FIRST SCHOOL in which we enroll, and the most important one in shaping our future, is our home. A casual view of modern television programs might lead us to believe that parents don't matter. I contend that nothing matters more.

When Benjamin West was a boy, his mother left him in charge of his younger sister, Sally. Benjamin found bottles of colored ink and painted Sally's portrait. When his mother arrived home, she discovered spilled ink and ruined paper. But before she had the opportunity to raise her voice and scold Benjamin, she saw the picture. Then she planted an encouraging kiss on his cheek. Benjamin West would later say, "My mother's kiss made me a painter."

Every child's life is like a book of blank pages waiting to be written on. Something is written each day. A parent who exposes a child to hours of television, video games, unsupervised time on the Internet, and an occasional trip to church is not likely to raise a child whose value system will mirror that of the parent. The child will probably reflect the value system of the entertainment industry.

While researching for an earlier book I cowrote on juvenile violence, *Kids Who Kill*,[1] I became aware that children need parents who are informed, involved, and invasive in their children's lives. There is no single fact that will explain why a child as young as eleven years old would commit mass murder. But one thing seems certain. The likelihood of this taking place decreases drastically when children have a stable home, good role models, and parents who are clearly more afraid *for* their children than afraid *of* their children.

Too many parents fear angering or alienating their children. They convince themselves that it is love that avoids asking their children questions about how their time is spent and who their friends are. They fool themselves into thinking they are being good parents when they don't hold their children accountable for their schoolwork and other activities. On the other hand, we are not to be "helicopter" parents who are so overprotective that our children turn into a generation of "snowflakes" who cannot learn through their failures or develop a healthy maturity and independence.

The requirement of parents summed up in Ephesians 6:4 is simple yet profound: "Do not exasperate your children; instead, bring them up in the training and instruction of the Lord." Children should not be driven to exasperation by parents who make demands that are so difficult to achieve that the children are prevented from succeeding. There is a vast difference between breaking a child's rebellious will and breaking his or her spirit.

As parents, our goal should be to channel the energy of our children rather than destroy their creative and curious natures given by God that motivates them to discover their unique purposes. We are further admonished to bring up our children "in the training and instruction of the Lord." By both example and exhortation, parents are to nourish their children. Most values are caught and then taught. Our children are more likely to imitate what they see us do than what they hear us say.

Training Our Replacements

I will always remember an incident that occurred during my years as a pastor when my children were young. One day, upon hearing loud voices in the living room, I peered around the corner to observe my three children, ranging at the time from ages three to nine, "playing church." They acted out a church service, including the singing, the preaching, and the important "taking the offering."

> By both example and exhortation, parents are to nourish our children. Most values are caught and then taught.

I was amused, but I also was struck by the realization that whether I liked it or not, my children were growing up to imitate me. Years later, I would be gratified when each of my three children indicated an interest in politics and government—although at times I wished they hadn't! It's a brutal business.

Our ultimate job as parents is to train our replacements. If we left our children a million shares of a valuable stock but did not leave them instructions on how to parent the next generation, how could we claim success? Our children do not need to be forced into proper behavior by being bullied to the point that they act out of terror rather than a desire to please.

A prison once offered each of the inmates a Mother's Day card so they could have the opportunity to write a loving greeting to their mothers. Within a short time, every card was taken. The effort was such a success that the warden decided he would also provide Father's Day cards. But as Father's Day neared, not one card was taken. This fact is revealing if you are searching for the causes of an ever-expanding prison population. This country is plagued by disappearing dads.

When a father views his role as little more than a baby maker, it is doubtful he will take the time or expend the effort to nurture a child into a healthy, balanced adult. Some of my most painful memories in counseling young children was hearing children as young as five years old blaming themselves for their parents' divorce. Too many children become convinced that their parents' inability to get along was because of them.

During the past few generations, children have gone from being an economic asset to an economic liability. We have moved from being an economy based largely on agriculture to an economy based on industry and technology. In an agricultural society, children were farmhands. Each child had a role to play in the success of the family enterprise. Yet today's children have little responsibility for the success of the household. Too many of them hear how much they are costing rather than how much they are worth.

Children should grow up with various tasks to perform that contribute to the success of the family. This gives a sense of worth to each family member. It also gives parents the opportunity to praise their children as they reach their goals.

Children imitate their parents even when they do not understand what they are copying or the consequences of their actions. I noticed this when my daughter, Sarah, was about two years old. I have always been an avid reader. One evening while seated in a recliner with my daughter on my lap, I was reading a book. She had one of her small picture books. To help turn the pages in my book, I would lick a finger in order to get a good grip on the page being turned.

> Children should grow up with various tasks to perform that contribute to the success of the family.

After a few minutes, I looked at my daughter, who had decided to "read" her book. As her right hand reached out to turn the page, she carefully licked a finger on her left hand. She wasn't sure why she was doing this. It never occurred to her to use the moistened finger on the page. But somehow, licking a finger was important to her dad when he was reading, and therefore it was important to her. Sarah has grown up to be known for "licking the sticky" out of the White House press corps in her job as press secretary to President Donald Trump.

One of the most difficult challenges is knowing when children are ready to be entrusted with higher levels of responsibility. A young boy came home from his first day of school. His father was eager to hear about his son's first day of kindergarten until the child stunned him with the question, "Dad, what is sex?"

The father thought, *I know kids are being exposed to sex at a much earlier age, but I wasn't expecting to have to explain the facts of life quite so soon!* Then he took a deep breath and said, "Son, sit down. I will do my best to explain." After he felt he had done a respectable job in explaining what sex was, he asked his son, "Did that help?" The boy replied, "I guess so. That was all very interesting. But a form we got at school today asked what sex I am. I just needed to know if I'm an M or an F."

In today's confused world, the child might not even know this is a binary choice of male or female. He might go to a school that tells five- and six-year-olds that they have over fifty choices of genders. And we wonder why kids today are utterly bewildered!

The Lesson of Being Patient

One of the most important lessons we can teach our children is to be patient when waiting for the things that are really important. Perhaps no lesson is more challenging for a parent to explain than that things of great value sometimes take a great amount of time.

When I was eleven years old, I received my first guitar for Christmas. My parents had saved money for months to buy an electric guitar from the J. C. Penney catalog. The guitar and small amplifier cost a whopping ninety-nine dollars in 1966. It was one of the happiest and most memorable experiences of my life. Like every other kid my age, I was convinced I could become the fifth Beatle or perhaps be the leader of a famous rock band, traveling the world and entertaining the masses. I soon discovered, however, that learning to play that guitar took work.

Today, that mail-order guitar sits in the Old State House in downtown Little Rock as part of a collection of memorabilia from governors. For many who come and see it, it probably represents little more than a kid's dream to be a musician. For me, though, it is a reminder that long before I ever played before an audience and heard the applause, I spent hours and hours in my room hearing only the complaints of a family whose members had to endure the throbbing sounds of an amplifier turned up as loud as it would go. Too bad I didn't listen to their pleas to "Turn it down!" I now deal with a hearing loss that is not debilitating but frustrating, brought on by years of music at full volume.

> One of the most important lessons we can teach our children is to be patient when waiting for the things that are really important.

We live in a world where a meal can be microwaved in seconds, and an Internet message can be transmitted around the world almost instantly. But part of the legacy we must leave is raising children who understand that some things can't be rushed. Things of great value take time. Patience is a virtue as well as a pathway to victory.

QUESTIONS FOR REFLECTION AND DISCUSSION

1. Why is it important that children grow up with various tasks to perform that contribute to the success of the family?

2. Do you think children need parents? Why or why not? What purpose do parents serve and what role do they play in the lives of their children?

3. Do you agree or disagree with the author's statement in referring to parents and children: "Most values are caught and then taught"? Explain your answer.

4. What evidence do you see of this statement by the author: "This country is plagued by disappearing dads"?

5. What legacy did your parents leave you? Describe the legacy that you would like to pass along to those who come behind you.

8

THE FAITH FACTOR

"I TRIED FAITH, but it just didn't work for me."

It's an excuse I've heard hundreds of times in hundreds of ways. It's sometimes expressed like this: "I've tried to forgive, but I just can't. I've tried my best to love him, but it just isn't happening."

Our culture has taught us to be in a hurry. We order our food from a car window and eat it from a paper sack as we hurry to our next appointment, driving as fast as the traffic will allow. We demand that our computers run at the speed of light and take it personally if our airline flights are more than five minutes late. We barely remember the days when popcorn was popped by holding a pan over a hot stove and shaking it vigorously. We prefer a three-minute zap in the microwave.

One of the most compelling verses in the New Testament is James 1:3: "The testing of your faith produces perseverance." Deep distortions have been made when it comes to the meaning of those simple words. But they mean just what they say. In order for faith to work, we have to test it. We probably will not do too well when we test it the first time and therefore will be forced to test it again and again.

During my teenage years and early adulthood, I longed for a faith that would catapult me above the pressures and problems of daily life. I believed real faith would either remove the problems from me or remove me from the problems. It seemed logical that if I pledged my love to God, then I would be able to escape flat tires, sick kids, surly store clerks, bad hair days, and severe indigestion after a large plate of enchiladas.

Somehow it never worked. I now realize that the sun shines on the just and unjust alike, and it also rains on the good as well as the bad (Matthew 5:45).

If we are members of the human family, then we will face trials and testing. Such tests are necessary, not because God needs to figure us out (he already knows what we are made of and how we will respond), but so he might reveal to us what we are about.

Consider It Joy

The only way a boat can be tested is to be placed in the water. The only way a rope can be tested is to be pulled. A bird does not test its wings by submitting to an analysis by an engineer but by leaving the nest and attempting to fly.

The book of James says that we can "consider it pure joy" (James 1:2) when we face such trials in life. This verse does not encourage us to enter into a type of emotional denial. On the contrary, it admonishes us to consider the joy of the ultimate outcome. Each trial we face is not an end in itself but a pathway to deeper character and to the ability to do things we have never done before.

A man passing by a friend asked, "How are you?" His friend replied, "Not too bad under the circumstances." The man asked, "Well, what are you doing under there?"

Indeed, we weren't designed to live "under the circumstances" but to get through the circumstances by living above and beyond them. The purpose of any test is not to make us fall but to make us fly. The results of our tests are never a surprise to God, but they are often a surprise to us. Many people have said after watching a close friend go through a trauma, "I feel so sorry for her. I just don't know how she does it. I could never maintain my faith in the midst of such tragedy."

> Each trial we face is not an end in itself but a pathway to deeper character and to the ability to do things we have never done before.

None of us believes we can endure crises and problems until after we've actually endured them. The test wasn't particularly revealing to the Creator, who knows us so well that the hairs on our head are numbered. The purpose of trials is to help us know just how much faith we have—to understand just how much tugging we can take before the tether breaks.

Try Your Faith

The book of James exhorts us to test—or try—our faith (1:3). It means just that. We try loving, we try forgiving, we try believing—and we will probably not be very good at it the first several hundred times we try.

Several years ago, I was invited to speak to a group of young adults at a ski resort in New Mexico. Many of my friends had told me what a wonderful experience skiing would be, and I was looking forward to it. After falling off the lift, having to climb uphill, and spending most of the day tumbling through the snow, I concluded I was not called to be a professional skier! In fact, I promised God that if I lived through that day, I would never try skiing again.

That was more than forty years ago, and I'm proud to say I've kept my promise! Since that time, I've had numerous invitations to go skiing. I try to make it very clear that I tried skiing and it's just not for me, and I would never want to break my promise to God.

My daughter, Sarah, is the youngest of our three children, and she is now married and the mother of three out of the six cutest children in the world. (The other three belong to my middle son and his wife.) It seems like only yesterday that she was learning to walk. Since she was the youngest, she could look around and see every family member walking. From her position crawling on the floor, she could easily observe how legs moved. I remember the day, when after months of observation, she concluded it was time to take her first step.

She pulled herself up by the edge of a sofa and carefully pushed off to begin her first steps. There was glee in her eyes as she took her first step and part of another before crashing with her nose buried in the carpet.

She crawled to a corner of the room and, with her arms folded, looked up at me and said in a clear voice, "Dad, I tried walking, and it just doesn't work for me. I realize you, Mom, John Mark, and David can all walk, but as you can see, I tried and I can't do it. I've studied it for months. I've given it my best effort. I wanted to, but you saw the results. I tried and failed. I can't walk. You'll have to carry me for the rest of my life."

Do you really believe that happened? Of course it didn't. The truth is that she tried again and again. Again she failed. Again she tried. This continued until she was so exhausted she fell asleep on the floor. The next day, she began the process again. Little by little, her one step became two and then three. It wasn't long before she was able to wobble all the way across the room. Then she was running, jumping, and going faster than her mother and me.

I remember my own childhood and the painful memories of learning to ride a bicycle. Other kids in the neighborhood who were older were already riding bicycles. I decided that if they could do it, then so could I. With great determination, I mounted the bicycle and fell. I fell numerous times trying to get the right balance. No matter how many times I scraped my elbows, I kept trying because I was determined to ride that bike.

Most of the things we do successfully in life come about because we're willing to try more than once. Whether it is walking, riding a bicycle, forgiving, loving, or believing, we rarely succeed on our first try. Many of us will experience far more failures than successes. We'll become what we practice being. If we practice being loving, caring, faithful, giving, and forgiving, then we'll become like that. If we practice selfishness, impatience, rudeness, greed, anger, and lust, then we can rest assured that we will become like that as well.

The Bible urges us to try our faith, but it also reminds us that when we try our faith, we become overcomers and conquerors. We're encouraged to ask questions so we may understand what we're experiencing and why. Some of the best news in the Bible is that God urges us to ask questions. James 1:5 says, "If any of you lacks wisdom, you should ask God, who gives generously to all without finding fault, and it will be given to you."

Know What You Don't Know

An important leadership lesson I learned and certainly found useful when I served as governor and was responsible for dozens of staff members, scores of cabinet heads and agency officials, and tens of thousands of state employees, was this: the person who will cause the most trouble is the person who doesn't know what he doesn't know. Not knowing how to do something can be remedied by training, but the arrogance of not admitting a lack of knowledge can be dangerous.

> We'll become what we practice being. If we practice being loving, caring, faithful, giving, and forgiving, then we'll become like that.

Knowledge is knowing what to do, but wisdom is knowing why and what next. God invites us to ask questions so we might develop wisdom and understanding. Yet many of us make the common mistake of being content to ask God for information rather than asking him for wisdom.

When my oldest son, John Mark, was about three years old, he managed to get a big splinter in his foot. I looked at his foot and told him I would remove the splinter. The next several minutes were some of the most unpleasant I've ever experienced as a parent. John Mark screamed, fought, pleaded, and resisted. I did my best to explain that removing the splinter would not be painful unless he moved his foot abruptly, causing me to stab the tweezers into his heel.

> Knowledge is knowing what to do, but wisdom is knowing why and what next. God invites us to ask questions so we might develop wisdom and understanding.

Although John Mark had the information he needed, he lacked confidence in my ability to remove the splinter. As a result, he was doing the very thing that was causing him pain. For a while, I thought we would either have to amputate his foot or have him put under a general anesthetic to bring this nightmare to a conclusion!

Sometimes we have information about God, but if we lack confidence in that information we will struggle, resist, and do great damage to ourselves trying to get away from an experience. It is precisely for this reason that God wants us to ask him for wisdom. We're free to ask him questions and expect answers. We're told that God will give us his wisdom "generously" (James 1:5). God gives us wisdom without asking for anything in return, and he will not belittle us for asking.

There is a caveat to this invitation. In fact, it is more of a condition. James 1:6 says if we ask, we must ask in faith and must not waver. Real faith is when we commit to following God's instructions before we even know what they are. We must have confidence in God rather than ourselves. This brings about a sense of peace and the capacity to be an overcomer. Although salvation is a one-time event, we do not become confident believers as a result of one unique experience. We become people of faith and perseverance by trying and then trying again and again.

Practice Makes Perfect

We've all heard the adage, "Practice makes perfect." That's true of virtually any discipline in life, whether playing the piano or forgiving people who have hurt us. We practice and then practice some more. Finally, what was once a struggle that required every ounce of concentration becomes so much a part of us that we do it with the effortless ease of a gold-medal figure skater.

Rest assured that no person starts the journey to championship with thousands of people cheering and a gold medal draped around his or her neck. There are thousands of painful falls on cold ice. The bystanders chuckle at the failures and never imagine that one day, the last laugh will belong to the person on the ice, who through faith and perseverance will finally stand on the middle podium with a gold medal listening to the "Star-Spangled Banner."

QUESTIONS FOR REFLECTION AND DISCUSSION

1. Describe an experience you have been through in which your faith was put to the test.

2. What do you think it means for a Christian to live "above the circumstances"?

3. What's the difference between asking God for information and asking him for wisdom?

4. In your opinion, what does it mean for a Christian believer to "try" his or her faith?

5. According to the author, we live in a society that expects instant results. In what ways does this attitude influence our thinking about faith?

9

FAITH WITH
A FUTURE

SUCCESSFULLY DRIVING A CAR involves paying attention not only to what you see through the windshield but also to what you see in the rearview mirror. While the windshield covers the front of the vehicle and allows you to see what is ahead, the rearview mirror is only a small piece of glass that gives you the ability to see what is behind.

There is a lesson here. While it is important to glance in the rearview mirror from time to time, it's more important to keep our eyes focused on the path ahead. A person who fails to glance at the past is in danger of losing perspective and perhaps being overcome by the unexpected. But a person who looks constantly at the past and fails to pay attention to the road ahead is destined for collision and disaster.

Part of a life done well is understanding where we were, where we are, and how important both of those are in determining where we're going. Savoring the successes of the past can be satisfying, but we must not camp out in the comfort of memories. Many aspiring college students flunk out because they believe their success in high school will lead to automatic success at the university level. The dedication and perseverance it took to turn the tassel at high school graduation is intensified in college.

I've observed many people who peaked in their late teens. They believed all the compliments showered on them by well-meaning people who told them they could sing like Mariah Carey or throw a football like Tom Brady. It's sad to see people whose best moments were wearing their high school letter jackets, so now in their forties they still try to fit into them, much like Uncle Rico in the hilarious movie *Napoleon Dynamite.*

> Part of a life done well is understanding where we were, where we are, and how important both of those are in determining where we're going.

Imagine how ridiculous it would be for me to assume that because I took an aspirin last week, I don't have to worry about a headache today. Even more absurd is the notion that after sixty-three years of breathing and having my heart keep me alive, I could give my lungs and heart the day off as a reward for their years of faithful, consistent labor. I would be dead within minutes after my heart stopped beating and my lungs quit functioning.

Successfully having done anything yesterday means absolutely nothing when it comes to successfully doing something today or tomorrow.

Leave Dead Things Buried

Many people hope their past successes in business relationships and even their successes in spiritual devotion to God can be translated into success tomorrow. The moment I stop exercising those disciplines of life, I stop growing and start dying. Genuine faith does not allow me to consider the disciplines of life to be an event. They're an ongoing process. Past successes guarantee nothing when it comes to future endeavors. If that were the case, my having won repeated elections at the state level would have made me president today!

By the same token, while some of us need to forget our past successes, others need to forget our past failures. No person is a failure because he failed. A failure is a person who stops trying. Failing at one thing is often what opens the door for other opportunities that would never have come our way had we not ventured down a road that our critics saw as failure but God used as a connecting point. Many people are paralyzed not because of their inability to perform but due to their unwillingness to stop staring at the road behind them and start looking at the road ahead.

Are there failures in your past? Go ahead and take a look at them. Then put your eyes on the road ahead, shift to drive, and hit the accelerator.

Our past sins and mistakes can't be changed. Some will leave scars on us as well as others. I have tire marks on my back from the people who betrayed me or lied to my face. But after we have made responsible efforts to right wrongs, make restitution, and ask the forgiveness of those we've hurt and offended, we need to leave dead things buried.

My family once had a parakeet named Cookie. I'm not sure how long Cookie had been in our family; it was as far back as I could remember. When I was about four years old, Cookie died. My sister and I decided Cookie deserved a proper burial. We took an old shoebox, turned it into a casket, and conducted an impressive funeral service. We carefully dug a grave in our backyard, placed the shoebox containing Cookie in the grave, and covered it with dirt to bring closure to our relationship with this family fixture.

After a few weeks, my four-year-old curiosity could not be contained. I wondered how Cookie was getting along in her underground habitat. Without seeking counsel from my older sister, I took it upon myself to do some digging. To this day, I remember my horror at seeing the condition of that bird several weeks after what I thought was a proper burial. As bad as Cookie's death had been, digging her up only made it worse.

Once we've confessed our sins, received forgiveness, and cleared the air as best we can, it's time to determine that we'll never go back and dig up what is dead. Digging up the sins and failures of the past will be unimaginably bad. We cannot allow our past experiences to intrude on our present experiences. If we do, our legacy will amount to little more than painful memories and lost opportunities.

Forgiveness and Restoration
Empower Our Present

Most people do things they regret. But you don't have to struggle with intense guilt over past failures. Guilt robs you of the energy you need to carry on the duties of today. In essence, guilt is using up today's resources on past actions. God never intended us to be overwhelmed with energy-draining guilt. This is why he made provisions for forgiveness and restoration. Forgiveness and restoration do more than cleanse our past; they empower our present.

During my first year as a pastor in Pine Bluff, Arkansas, I received a book from a major publishing company. I had not ordered the book, and there was neither a bill nor an explanation for the shipment. I assumed it was a promotional gift from the publisher sent to pastors in hopes they would buy an additional twelve books in the series.

> Forgiveness and restoration do more than cleanse our past; they empower our present.

The following month, the second book in the series arrived. Again, there was neither a bill nor an explanation. The third month, the third book arrived. This time there was a bill for all three books. Since I had not ordered the series, I was confident it was a mistake. I wrote the publishing house, informing them I would be happy to return the books if they would send me a shipping label and instructions for proper return.

My next contact with the company was when the fourth book in the series arrived. Thinking my letter had not gotten there in time to stop the fourth book, I waited. The fifth month saw another book arrive.

I wrote the publisher again and asked for a shipping label so I could return all five books. The next month, I received a sixth book and a bill for all books in the series thus far. I sent a third letter. You guessed it. In the seventh month, I got the seventh book and a bill for all seven books. This time, the billing letter was more aggressive. I was now receiving past-due notices for books I had never ordered and had repeatedly tried to return.

I mailed yet another letter, but the eighth and ninth months resulted in the eighth and ninth books in the thirteen-month series being sent. I tried several long-distance telephone calls. Each time, I was assured the situation would be corrected. By the time the twelfth book arrived, my account had been turned over to a collection agency, which threatened harsh action if I didn't pay the publisher immediately for books I had never ordered and seemed unable to return.

I made one final try. A little research yielded the name of the president of the publishing company. I wrote him a letter in which I outlined the one-year saga and my futile attempts to get someone's attention at his company. I added that my church spent thousands of dollars each year purchasing literature. If this was how the company operated, I told him, then I would do my best to ensure my church and any other churches I could contact avoided doing business with the company.

Less than a week later, my secretary informed me the gentleman to whom I had written the letter was on the phone. Considering my past dealings with the company, I wasn't sure if he was calling to correct the situation or to announce that he was sending two goons over to rearrange my face.

Much to my relief, he apologized profusely and indicated that his own research had found the many errors on their part. After he acknowledged I had ordered nothing and therefore owed nothing, he told me to keep the entire series of thirteen books. In addition, he would also send a commentary set I had long wanted but couldn't afford. He said if I had problems with his company again to simply use his name and ask that any questions be directed to him.

> When we think we can't handle the guilt any longer, our best course is to quit trying to confront it ourselves and to take it directly to the top.

Two days later, a twenty-volume commentary arrived. It remains one of my most frequently used resource materials. The company's president was true to his word. I was never billed for the thirteen-book series or the commentary set.

In a sense, guilt is being billed for sins we either didn't commit, have already paid for, or don't have the resources to pay for. Guilt drains us of faith, energy, and hope. When we think we can't handle the guilt any longer, our best course is to quit trying to confront it ourselves and to take it directly to the top.

When we take our problems to God, not only is he willing to take care of them, but he does something even more wonderful. He tells us if we are ever overburdened with guilt again that we should not attempt to deal with it by ourselves. We are to refer everything to him and allow him to deal with it. Ridding us of strength-robbing guilt by giving us faith with a future is one of God's greatest gifts.

QUESTIONS FOR REFLECTION AND DISCUSSION

1. In what ways does understanding our past help us better understand the present and chart our future course?

2. What happens to people when they stop learning and choose instead to live off their accomplishments in the past?

3. What do you think the author means by this statement: "Guilt is using up today's resources on past actions"? Have you ever experienced this in your own life? If so, describe the situation.

4. Is there some past failure in your life that you need to put behind you? What specific things can you do to move beyond your failures and mistakes?

5. How does God's forgiveness and restoration cleanse our past and empower our present?

10

FAITH IS
A PROCESS

REAL FAITH IS NOT ONLY getting beyond our past: it's recognizing that faith is an ongoing process. None of us has "arrived." At best, we can say we're "on the way." A big mistake many people make is believing that at some point in the future we will be complete and thus relieved from the prospect of additional construction. That is not and will never be the case on this side of eternity.

Years ago, I attended a seminar sponsored by the Institute in Basic Life Principles. Their seminars have helped millions of people cope with the practical issues of living a life of faith. At the completion of the seminar, I was given a button on which this message appeared: "PBPGINFWMY" We were told to keep that message in mind. It stands for, "Please Be Patient; God Is Not Finished with

Me Yet." What a wonderful reminder that while I'm not everything I want to be, I'm not all the things I once was!

Faith That Motivates

Our lives are filled with pressure and stress. This is not necessarily bad. Stress and tension, properly balanced, give us strength. A muscle never stretched and tested will become useless, but one that is stretched too far will tear and leave you writhing in pain.

In 2003, after my doctor sat me down and gave me "the talk" about taking better care of myself, I set forth on an aggressive effort to regain my health. I lost 110 pounds and did something I had not done since I was in elementary school—I started running. When I was nine, I ran to get away from bullies. At age forty-seven, I began to run toward something (health).

I was so proud of myself when I ran the Firecracker Fast 5K in Little Rock, held on the Fourth of July in 2004. Shortly thereafter, I was paid a visit by the organizers of the Little Rock Marathon, who asked me to consider running their marathon the next year. I thought they were absolutely nuts. It's one thing to run a 5K, which is about 3.1 miles. A marathon is 26.2 miles! They assured me that it was possible because it's all about training and gaining—training faithfully and gaining capacity each week. Frankly, I started the training not because I thought I could do it, but because I wanted to show them that I couldn't and figured that once I got to where I could run five miles or so without completely collapsing, they would leave me alone.

As I trained each week, I built a new level of capacity. One of the greatest days of my life was crossing the finish line at the Little Rock

Marathon in March 2005. I ended up doing four full marathons before a knee injury ended what I'm sure would have been an epic running career. But preparing for and running marathons taught me something. Of course I learned about the fundamentals of running, but more importantly, I learned some things about myself.

Faith That Empowers

The submarine is an amazing vessel. It would collapse like a paper cup under the extraordinary pressure placed on its hull if not for the internal pressure that equalizes the pressure from outside. Faith in our lives does not exempt us from external pressure. Faith ensures that the power of the living God through Jesus Christ works from the inside to equalize the outside pressure, giving us strength and keeping us from collapsing like a paper cup.

Real faith involves having something in the distance to motivate us and keep us moving, as the apostle Paul admonished in his letter to the Philippians. We should "press on toward the goal" (Philippians 3:14). Imagine an Olympic swimmer as he propels his body forward, stretching his chest, giving every ounce of energy to reach the goal.

There is nothing unholy about wanting to be a winner. The opposite is true: there is a great deal unholy about *not* wanting to be a winner. One of the most inspiring films I've seen is *Chariots of Fire*, the true story of Olympic champion Eric Liddell. Eric was a devout Christian, but he never thought of his faith as something that would cause him

> Faith gives us a focus for our future, helps us move toward our destiny, and provides us the capacity to continue working toward a life done well.

11

WINNING
AN ELECTION,
LOSING
A GENERATION

POLITICS IS A CONTACT SPORT. It has increasingly become a
demolition derby, with each contestant entering the arena and then
engaging in a series of crashes. Whoever remains standing is declared the winner. The best person with the superior ideas is often
less important than the most creative advertising campaign and the
largest war chest. Add in the cynicism of the media and the fact
that so many political opponents are willing to play hardball, and
this means that running for public office is certainly not for the faint
of heart. I have often said, "If you can't stand the sight of your own
blood, then politics is not the game for you."

I may not always like the process of politics, but the end product is often a public policy that lays the track on which the next generation will move forward. No matter how idealistic you are when entering the political arena, I can attest from personal experience there's always a temptation to make decisions that will affect the next election rather than chart the best course for the next generation. It's easy to justify such an attitude by telling yourself that if you don't get reelected, then you won't be able to have an impact on future policy development. Our society increasingly demands measurable results in a short time. Being in public office is now about building a *résumé* of accomplishments rather than laying the foundation for a lasting legacy that will result in a lifetime of change.

When I was governor of Arkansas, I visited public schools, preferably elementary schools, as often as possible. One of my primary reasons for visiting schools was not so much to introduce the students to a governor as it was to remind me of what was really important about being in public office. To this day, my batteries are recharged when I'm around children who are still filled with awe and wonder. They have not become like so many adults—angry, distrustful, and filled with doubt and broken dreams. I especially love spending time with my grandchildren, although at times I wonder, and even worry, about their future.

Not long after becoming governor in 1996, I sat in a meeting room at a Little Rock hospital with almost fifty representatives of organizations that received Medicaid funds. We had asked them to assist us in finding areas in which we could save money in the Medicaid system. The state was rapidly approaching the point at which the needs would exceed the funding levels.

I listened for more than an hour as participants talked about the virtues of their organizations and why they needed to be given even more money. In a meeting designed to ask the participants how they could live with less, each found a way to articulate how they couldn't live without more.

Then I called on a quiet lady across the room who lifted her hand to be recognized. What she said in the next few minutes stirred something in me that would change my views and the agenda for tens of thousands of Arkansas children. She was Amy Rossi, executive director of Arkansas Advocates for Children and Families. She was known by regulars at the state capitol as a well-meaning person who tried to influence legislation to have a more positive effect on children, especially those from poor families.

I had heard from people who wanted more tax dollars for their organizations, but Rossi's plea was refreshingly different. She wasn't there to ask for more money for an organization. She was there to remind us of a serious need in our state. She spoke passionately about the 110,000 Arkansas children whose parents were working and avoiding welfare but whose incomes were not enough to afford adequate health insurance for their children.

These kids fell into an unfair trap. Their parents earned too much to qualify for the platinum program of Medicaid, which covered pretty much everything at no cost to the recipient, but not enough to afford quality private health insurance plans. These were children whose chronic illnesses often were going undiagnosed and untreated.

Amy Rossi's plea might have been filed away with the other good ideas I regularly heard as governor, but I couldn't stop thinking about those children. I realized the only thing that separated them and me was forty years. When I was young, my parents would have qualified for Medicaid, but they for sure couldn't have afforded the kind of health-care costs being faced by families in the mid-1990s. Fortunately for me and my own children, the cost of insurance and medical care was not nearly as high in the 1950s and 1960s as it was in the 1990s. It occurred to me that many children perhaps were being penalized because their parents had worked their way above the poverty line.

Subsequent meetings with the director of the Arkansas Department of Human Services, Tom Dalton, and State Medicaid Director Ray Hanley brought forth a simple but revolutionary idea that gave preventative health care to the children of working parents. The ARKids First program was born. I introduced it to the Arkansas legislature in January 1997. It passed without a negative vote in either the House or the Senate. I assure you, it was one of the few things I ever proposed in almost eleven years as governor that had that kind of unanimous support!

I remember coming up with the name of the program while seated at my desk at the state capitol, feeling a true sense of inspiration. When the legislation was approved, I had the pleasure of signing the bill while seated at a small table surrounded by children at a downtown Little Rock daycare center. The children were drawing pictures with crayons.

As I prepared to sign the bill, I reached for one of the crayons and probably made history by being the first person to sign a bill into law with a crayon rather than a pen. The spontaneity of the moment took hold, and the crayon became one of the symbols of the plan.

Since its conception in 1997, the ARKids First program has been incredibly successful, insuring more than seventy thousand children whose families probably could not have otherwise afforded preventive health care. By the time Congress passed its own children's health initiative months later, our program was up and running. Many of our citizens actually welcomed the small copayment that was required since it gave them a sense of shared responsibility and a feeling of not being on welfare.

ARKids First has proven that it is less expensive to prevent a problem than it is to try to fix it once it has grown into something much larger. The value of ARKids First has been even easier to see during the past two decades as thousands of children have grown up not having missed school because of chronic illnesses. Is the program costly? It's not as costly as having large numbers of sick children who miss class, can't hear the teacher, see the board, or have a stomachache and can't concentrate.

Another initiative we promoted heavily in Arkansas was the Smart Start program, which put a major emphasis on high standards and accountability while focusing on reading, math, and character-based education in the early grades. With Arkansas ranked near the bottom in educational achievement, creating and implementing a statewide initiative that refocused public education was an important task.

Like the ARKids First program, we knew the real value of Smart Start would not be evident by the next election. It took several years to see what happened when children grew up in a public education system where the standards were raised instead of lowered, where individual students and schools were held accountable. Looking back now, we can see that the state's test scores dramatically improved and it did make a difference. I learned from these successful programs that we can truly make a difference when we choose to keep our focus on the ultimate good, and not merely on immediate results.

Short-Term Splash, Long-Term Loss

There is a temptation among public officials to implement programs with an eye toward short-term results. This is an age of launching "micro-policies" that provide colorful backdrops for television cameras. Though they begin with a splash, most of these programs do little in the long run to improve our country.

The longer I served as governor, the more I tried to remind myself that my most important decisions were not the ones that would affect the next election but those that would affect the next generation. If public officials had fought for generational programs fifty years ago, then my state might not have been one of the poorest in the country. The politics of "right now" too often robs citizens of the changes needed to make their lives better.

Today, the Arkansas prison system is one of the most efficient in the country in terms of cost. During my tenure as governor, we spent an average of about $16,000 per year on each inmate, far below the national average. But consider that for the same amount of money we spent to keep someone in a prison, we could have enrolled a student in any college or university in the state at the time—paying full tuition plus room and board, buying books, and still providing some spending money. Few things grieve me more than having to build more prisons to meet the demand that drugs and crime have placed on the Arkansas Department of Correction.

I can't help but wonder how many people who languish in our prisons today might have been learning in our colleges and universities if we had been more proactive when they were children. If we had placed a higher priority on building a fence at the top of the hill to keep them from falling off, then we wouldn't have had to spend big money on ambulances at the bottom of the hill to pick up what was left after they fell.

> The politics of "right now" too often robs citizens of the changes needed to make their lives better.

During my almost eleven years as governor, I was determined to resist the lure of instant gratification in order to dedicate my tenure in office to adopting policies that might not have an immediate result but would help the people of my state beyond my lifetime.

Making Decisions That Affect Others

Not everyone governs a state, I fully understand. But everyone makes decisions that affect others. Just as politicians are tempted to live only for the next election, many Americans live only for the next vacation or even the next weekend. In a culture that's addicted to pleasure and immediate gratification, it is increasingly difficult for us to live in a way that will impact lives long after we are gone.

As a young man approached his birthday, he could sense

something significant was going on. A week before his birthday party, he found the garage door locked. On his birthday, he was escorted to the kitchen, where he was met by his parents, grandparents, and a number of aunts and uncles. The family then gathered near the garage door and watched as the boy's father placed the key in the padlock and opened the door.

A large section of a tree—more than five feet tall and at least a foot thick—greeted the boy and his family. As he approached the tree, he noticed it had been meticulously polished. He also noticed small signs that noted the dates at which rings of the tree had formed and the connection to events in history. One ring was labeled "The Emancipation Proclamation, 1863." Another marker showed the year when his mother and father had married.

As the boy studied the rings, he learned about the history of his family and also gained clues about the history of his race. The boy had been given something far more valuable than a piece of a tree. This gift taught him about his past.

The boy's name was Alex Haley, who grew up to write the bestselling novel *Roots*. This book was adapted into the most significant television miniseries in our country's history.

As we work, raise our children, and make daily decisions, we need to ask if our choices are for the immediate or for the ultimate good. Imagine the difference if governments began to make decisions based on how they impact the next generation rather than how they influence the next election.

QUESTIONS FOR REFLECTION AND DISCUSSION

1. Should public officials strive for long-term solutions to problems or for immediate and short-term results? Explain your answer.

2. Why do you think the author declares that "running for public office is certainly not for the faint of heart"?

3. Why is it tempting to public officials to make short-term policy decisions rather than decisions that affect the next generation?

4. Why is it less expensive to prevent a problem than it is to try to fix it once it has grown into something much larger?

5. Have you ever made a decision that worked in the short term but turned out to be a bad decision several years down the road? What can you do to keep from making such shortsighted decisions in the future?

12

THE DITTO FACTOR

THE TRAIL WE LEAVE BEHIND IN LIFE is largely determined by the manner in which we lead. You don't have to be a governor to be in a position of leadership. Being a leader is not necessarily the same as being the chief executive officer of a major corporation, the president of a large club, or the chairman of a committee. Anyone who is a parent is a leader of perhaps the most important corporation of all—the family.

Biblical Requirements of Leadership

Through the years, I've attended many leadership courses and participated in a number of community leadership organizations. But rarely have I been confronted with anything that could not have been gleaned from a thorough reading of the book of Proverbs and the Sermon on the Mount. Let's examine some of the Bible's requirements for leaders.

Flee Youthful Lusts

Before we get in front of some things as leaders, we need to get away from others. The apostle Paul urged Timothy to "flee the evil desires of youth" (2 Timothy 2:22). This verse is often used to hammer away at teenagers about avoiding premarital sex, but the command is actually much larger in scope. To flee youthful lust means to run away from any impulse that is characteristic of immaturity. Such traits include impatience, quickness to argue, unrealistic ambitions, willingness to lose a war in order to win a battle, and rejection of tradition and experience. It can mean simply the know-it-all attitude.

While driving on the freeway one day, I spotted a bumper sticker that made me laugh out loud. It said, "Hire a teenager while he still knows everything."

It's irritating but totally predictable when a child asks on a long trip, "Are we there yet?" We expect children to argue about who sits near the window. And we're not surprised when young children argue the virtues of eating ice cream instead of vegetables. They might even contend that a daily bath is unnecessary, even when we can smell them before we see them.

While all of this might be predictable for a child, it is important to flee youthful lust as a person grows. This reminds me of the story of Jimmy Taylor, who refused to get out of bed one morning. He proclaimed, "I'm not going to school today. I hate school, and I'm not going back. The kids hate me, the teachers hate me, I hate the food, and I'm tired of being called names. Just give me one good reason I should go." Mrs. Taylor replied, "You're going to school today whether you want to or not, because you're forty-six years old—and you're the principal."

A mark of maturity is when we perform even unpleasant, mundane tasks with regularity and without complaint. A person who has to force himself out of bed to go to work each day is living a life that is mediocre, not done well. The person who has to be begged to perform basic responsibilities is acting like a child. When it comes to leadership, it is important that we run *from* some things before we run *to* some things.

Learn to Follow

Another paradox of leadership is that before leaders lead, they must learn to follow. Some wag has said, "The self-made man is the world's greatest example of unskilled labor." Following our instincts while ignoring our Creator is a foolish course.

One of the greatest mysteries of adolescence is how a fifteen-year-old can be pressed into smoking, drinking, reckless driving, and promiscuous activity through the urging of another teenager. The rational thing would be to follow those who have a successful track record. Would you be willing to put your life in the hands of a surgeon who has never performed the procedure you need?

When speaking to student groups, I often ask, "How many of you would like to go with me?" I usually get a lot of strange

> When it comes to leadership, it is important that we run *from* some things before we run *to* some things.

looks before someone finally asks, "Where are you going?" I have very few takers when I respond, "You'll just have to trust me." My point is to remind them that if they don't know where they're being led, it might be best not to follow.

One of the reasons it is rational to follow the Creator is that wherever he leads us, we can be assured he has been there before. He knows the path.

Forsake Arguments

Just as leaders need to flee certain activities, they also need to forsake arguments. While it is appropriate to ask questions to gain insight, we are not in a position to lead if our opportunities to move forward are hindered by an argumentative spirit.

There is a difference between asking questions and questioning everything. We all know someone who thinks every issue needs opposition. The person who argues about every decision and every opinion not only loses companionship but also loses the capacity to be a companion during a crisis. It's difficult to visit a hospital room and offer comfort to a person with whom you've been at odds on virtually every issue.

When we express an opinion, we must do so in the right spirit. Having a short temper and always being ready to fight is more than unbecoming of a leader. It is ultimately the undoing of a leader.

Lead by Loving, Not Shoving

We're told in the Scriptures to exercise "meekness" (Colossians 3:12 NKJV). But there is a difference between being meek and being weak. Meekness implies "teachability." A leader must have a proper balance between being fed knowledge and feeding knowledge and wisdom to others. We should lead by loving, not by shoving.

The real job of leaders is to make others successful rather than using others to make themselves successful. The art of bringing out the best in others will multiply your own capacity for success. Look around and notice that the most successful people you know tend to be those who have invested their lives in others. By helping those around them rise, leaders also succeed.

Lead by Example

True leaders never ask of others what they're unwilling to do themselves. The attitude of "feeding while we're leading" recognizes that a humble, teachable heart is a prerequisite to gaining the confidence of others.

Many people want to hear from God and be assured their life's plan is being carried out properly. One way to ensure we are acting under God's direction and not under our own power is by following the real lessons of leadership. When we do

> The real job of leaders is to make others successful rather than using others to make themselves successful.

that, we're more likely to have knowledge of the specific steps God wants us to take. It should be our goal to make God's plan known in word as well as spirit.

The Attitudes of Biblical Leadership

In the 1970s, I worked for James Robison, head of a global mission organization. While traveling to a speaking engagement, James handed me an article and asked me to pass it to his then-teenage daughter, Rhonda. Clowning around, I thrust the folder containing the article in front of Rhonda and said, "Here! Your dad said for you to read this."

James heard me and said, "Mike, I did ask you to give it to her, but I didn't tell you with that tone or spirit. It's not enough that you communicate what I said. It's equally important that you communicate it in the spirit in which I said it."

I learned a vital lesson that day. It's not enough for us to be right when we speak the truth. We must also speak the truth in the right spirit if we're genuinely interested in having God's Word revealed to us or if we're interested in correctly revealing it to others. We must say it in the manner the Father said it, lest we communicate the wrong message in the wrong spirit, bringing the wrong result.

> The effectiveness of our leadership will be determined by the number of people who come to a knowledge of God because of us and who do what's right.

Repentance may be an old-fashioned word, but it would do us all good to recognize the significance of turning from the things in our lives that hurt and hinder us. Real leadership will cause those around us to turn from what is wrong and toward what is right. Unfortunately, some people are more interested in winning arguments than winning converts to the correct course of action. But the Bible doesn't say, "He who wins arguments is wise." It says, "He who wins *souls* is wise" (Proverbs 11:30 NKJV).

The effectiveness of our leadership will be determined by the number of people who come to a knowledge of God because of us and end up doing what's right. Our effectiveness also will be determined by the number of people who reject God because of us and end up doing what's wrong. Good leadership will cause others to follow us down the proper path rather than down the road to rebellion.

As leaders, we will make some mistakes, and some of these will be quite harmful. True leadership gives us the capacity to help people recover from the traps into which they fall. It's not a disgrace when people stumble into a trap, but it's unacceptable when they are content to stay there.

We weren't designed by God to be taken captive by bad habits, attitudes, and behaviors that lead to our destruction. Leading others out of the darkness and into the light gives us the capacity to leave behind something greater than money or property. We leave behind better people.

QUESTIONS FOR REFLECTION AND DISCUSSION

1. Do you think it is important to flee youthful lust as a person grows? Why or why not?

2. What do you think it means to express an opinion in the right spirit? What do you think could happen when opinions are not expressed in a right spirit?

3. In what ways are you leading by example in your own life?

4. In your own words, describe the difference between meekness and weakness. Which one do you think is preferable? Would you describe yourself as weak or meek?

5. What do you think the author means by this statement: "It's not a disgrace when people stumble into a trap, but it's unacceptable when they are content to stay there"? Describe a time when you or someone you know was content to stay in a "trap."

Part Three

A LEGACY
LIVED

13

THE POWER OF BEING POSITIVE

ON MY WAY TO WORK YEARS AGO, I heard a catchy song on the radio. During the next several weeks, I heard it repeatedly. As it turned out, that song became a big hit, sold more than ten million copies, and was nominated for a Grammy. Over and over, the lyrics admonished us, "Don't worry, be happy!" Written and performed by Bobby McFerrin, the song had such an impact that the February 27, 1989 issue of *Newsweek* carried a two-page spread about its popularity. Bloomingdale's even opened a "Don't Worry, Be Happy" shop.

Being a positive person has been the focus of countless books, seminars, sermons, video series, and personal counseling sessions. If we're going to live a life that is done well, then we need to leave something that future generations would want to pick up and carry on. There is power in being positive, not only for the immediate but also for the ultimate.

One of the fallacies of the positive-thinking movement is that being a positive person consists of working up enough emotion to ignore reality and talk yourself into believing that everything will be fine. It's true that a positive spirit will take the unpleasant experiences of life and make them more tolerable. But there is something even better as it relates to the ultimate outcome of life.

Positive Principles

Our attitude does determine our altitude in many respects. If we believe we're going to succeed, we are much more likely to do so. If we are convinced we'll fail, we will rarely be disappointed in our prediction. There are some principles we can apply to unleash the power of being positive.

Being Positive Originates in a Peaceful Mind

Our thoughts really do control us. A Hindu trader once asked a missionary, "What do you put on your face to make it shine?" When the missionary realized he was talking about his countenance, he explained the "shine" came from the inside, not the outside. Our hearts experience; our faces reflect. When we are at peace with our inner selves, this peace is projected in our expressions. People who look for good are usually able to find it. Those who see the worst in everything generally project anger and bitterness.

People tend to be most critical of the success of others in areas where they are weak. For example, I have observed that people who give the least are the most vocal in criticizing how money is spent. People who do the least work most often criticize the work being done. Those who have the fewest friends are those who are the least friendly. The power of being positive originates in a peaceful mind.

Being Positive Is Articulated Through a Pleasant Mouth

Our words reveal our hearts just as our countenance reflects our spirit. When Frederick Kappel was the chief executive officer of AT&T, he grew weary of a talkative lady whose negative comments and questions dominated discussions. In the fourth hour of a stockholders' meeting, the lady asked Kappel how much money had been given to charities. Kappel answered, "About $10 [sic] million." The lady replied, "I'm about to faint . . ." Likely to the delight of the audience, Kappel responded, "That would be helpful."[1]

> The power of being positive originates in a peaceful mind.

What fills our minds generally flows from our mouths. When we have developed an attitude of being positive, it will be reflected in what we think as well as what we say.

Being Positive Circulates by Positive Methods

Acting with integrity is never out of style. Few of us respect a crook or a schemer. When it appears that a person of dubious character is succeeding, we are disappointed. We think it is a shame when a person achieves something good through bad deeds or behaviors.

advances the idea that it is not the personality as much as it is unresolved anger and hostility that puts stress on the human body.[5]

This philosophy of life proved to be especially helpful when I had a political career. During my tenure as governor, I tried to live by this motto: "Take God seriously, but don't take yourself too seriously." It's easy to do just the opposite, placing a great deal of importance on what we do, what we think, where we go, and what people think of us while paying little attention to our relationship with the God from whom we came and to whom we will return.

It is vitally important not only for our sense of legacy but also for our health that we take God seriously and lighten up about ourselves. The world was here before we came, and it will continue long after we are gone.

During my freshman year at Ouachita Baptist University in the fall of 1973, the outbreak of the Yom Kippur War in the Middle East caused many theology students to surmise this was the beginning of the end and that the world soon would face its final chapter.

One of my fellow freshmen scheduled an appointment with Dr. Vester Wolber, chairman of Ouachita's religion department, to announce he was withdrawing from school because he could not justify sitting in a classroom while there were so many souls to save before the world ended. Dr. Wolber, one of the wisest men I've known, leaned back in his chair, pulled his glasses down on his nose, and said to my classmate: "My, my, I'm not sure how the good Lord has gotten along all these years without you."

A healthy sense of humor is an important ingredient for a person whose legacy will be attractive and desirable.

The Blessings of Laughter

My father never made much money. He worked as a firefighter to pay the rent and keep food on the table. He had to take a second job as a mechanic on his days off from the fire station. With him and my mother working, we had just enough money to get by but never enough to get ahead. When my father died in 1996, about all he had to leave my mother in a material sense was a house, a small life insurance benefit, a few personal items, and a shed filled with tools.

But he left something else that was priceless. He left us with a wonderful sense of humor. It was hard to appreciate how laughter filled our house until I grew older and realized not everyone's home is blessed with such humor. It's not that his Irish temper didn't come through occasionally. But no matter how little we had, we always had a home filled with laughter.

> A healthy sense of humor is an important ingredient for a person whose legacy will be attractive and desirable.

The Bible tells us that we are created in God's image (Genesis 1:27). If we have a sense of humor, it is because our heavenly Father does as well. I'm convinced he has a wonderful sense of humor, as evidenced by some of the people he has created!

During my years as a pastor, I conducted more than four hundred funerals. I found that the careful use of humor at a funeral service could be helpful in bringing peace to a family and easing the tension that such an occasion can bring.

Some of the most often-prescribed drugs today are antidepressants. If we were to take the Bible at face value, we probably would discover that, in at least some cases, instead of reaching for medicine we would sometimes be better off reaching for a joke book. We might discover that humor really is healthy and adds to the power of being positive.

The Power of a Positive Spirit

Positive people are welcome in almost every situation. By contrast, negative people make us want to flee. A person known for a quick wit, a kind word, a smiling face, and a willingness to listen is a valuable asset. I've known some people who thought there was very little they had to offer the world. They weren't outstanding singers, they didn't have the capacity to speak eloquently, they weren't tremendous administrators, and they didn't exhibit leadership skills. But they did have a positive zeal for life. Their presence did more to light up a room than a floodlight.

There is power in a positive spirit. The person who has it and shares it is one who will leave a real legacy. You can be that person!

QUESTIONS FOR REFLECTION AND DISCUSSION

1. Have you ever known someone whom you considered a "negaholic"? Describe the characteristics of such a person.

2. According to the author, one characteristic of a leader is that he or she must be teachable. What is the most valuable lesson you have learned about life and leadership recently?

3. Why is it important for leaders to speak the truth as well as speak it in the right spirit?

4. Do you agree with this statement by the author: "A healthy sense of humor is an important ingredient for a person whose legacy will be attractive and desirable"? Why or why not?

5. Why is a know-it-all attitude a mark of immaturity? What are some additional characteristics of an immature person?

14

IT'S THE MONEY, HONEY

THE DENTIST HELD the narrow silver instrument with a needle-like probe at the end. I was already nervous. When the sharp probe touched my tooth cavity, every muscle in my body stiffened. I let out an audible noise and sat straight up in the chair despite the significant levels of nitrous oxide I was inhaling through a rubber mask over my nose.

"Did that hurt?" asked the dentist. I wanted to reply, "Hurt? Why no, it felt great. In fact, I was hoping you could do that several more times. I just screamed and sat up in the chair to make sure you were having as much fun as I am."

As sensitive as my tooth was, people are even more sensitive about money. They are especially sensitive about anyone who tries to convince them to give any of it up. As a pastor and a political candidate, I've spent a great deal of my adult life finding creative, not-so-painful methods of getting people to feel good about parting with their money in order to finance a cause.

During the 1992 presidential campaign, a sign hung in the Bill Clinton campaign headquarters in downtown Little Rock. Placed there by political consultant James Carville, the sign proclaimed, "It's the economy, stupid." Political analysts say the 1992 election, as well as every presidential election since then, was indeed more about people's attitudes toward the economy than any other issue.

Money not only drives elections; it also influences marriages, business relationships, and international relations. Our nation's prisons are filled with people who killed others or tried to kill them because they wanted money that was not theirs.

Part of a life done well depends on the manner in which we manage our money. We can gain a spiritual perspective on money by looking at our requirement and God's response.

Our Requirement

In the book of Malachi, God's people were told they had abandoned God's law and their disobedience had brought a curse so severe that crops were failing and the economy was collapsing. The people of Malachi's day were unsure what sin they had committed.

Mincing no words, the prophet told them they had robbed God (Malachi 3:8). Of course, it's impossible to rob God in a literal sense, but in the ancient Hebrew language the word means "to cover, i.e. (figuratively) defraud."[1] Because the people of Malachi's day had kept what they were supposed to give to God in tithes and offerings, they were experiencing an unusual economic downturn. The real issue was not money but obedience.

The prophet understood correctly that 90 percent obedience to God's command is 100 percent disobedience. The people were to tithe 10 percent of their earnings to God as a tangible expression of their trust and confidence in him. They needed to realize that having 90 percent of their income with God's blessing was far superior to having 100 percent of their income with his curse.

> The biblical concept of stewardship recognizes that you and I are not actually the owners of anything. We are mere managers of the things that are in our control.

The prophet urged the people to "bring the whole tithe into the storehouse" (Malachi 3:10) and further challenged them to prove if God was in fact faithful. Could God be trusted to bail them out of poverty if they had not trusted him with their prosperity? The idea of managing money revolves around being a responsible steward—or manager—of the resources we have been given by God. The biblical concept of stewardship recognizes that you and I are not actually the owners of anything. We are mere managers of the things that are in our control.

Stewardship is the proper management of the time, talent, and treasure that God has given us. When we recognize our role as stewards, we understand that God owns and orders all things. He has a right to tell us what to do with the property and possessions that he has entrusted to our management.

Before the steward can manage things, he must manage himself.

God's requirement for us to give generously is not because he is needy but because we are needy.

God's Response

Giving and receiving are directly proportionate. It's as simple as the law of the harvest: we reap what we sow. And not only is it true that we reap what we sow, but also that we reap later than we sow. Further, we reap more than we sow. A person who claims to want to be more like God is a person who should become as generous as possible. When we give our time, talent, and treasure, we most resemble the God whom we worship.

The one thing that is clear about our heavenly Father is that he has never tried to see how little he could get by with giving in order to meet the minimum requirements of being God. I've always worried about people who ask me what is the minimum they can give in order to meet what they believe to be God's demands.

Some people argue that the tithe is passé because it is part of the Old Testament law. But the Old Testament requirement to tithe was not abolished by New Testament grace. In fact, the command to tithe was affirmed by Jesus in the New Testament (Matthew 23:23; Luke 11:42). Grace always requires a greater devotion—not less devotion—than the law.

One of the remarkable surprises of the Bible is that we are told our giving should be "cheerful" (2 Corinthians 9:7). I've often quipped there are many similarities between politics and church work. Large amounts of money must be raised for each. The primary difference is that in church work, you preach that God loves a cheerful giver. But in politics, you will accept money from a grouch!

Giving with a smile and enthusiasm most resembles God, who never regrets the gifts he gives us. When we give like God, we are "source giving" rather than "sense giving." We give out of our understanding that God is the source of all we have rather than giving because it makes sense financially.

Our Giving Reveals Our Trust in God

Malachi told the people that giving would cause God to "rebuke the devourer" (Malachi 3:11 NKJV). The manner in which we handle money doesn't reveal as much about the quantity of our finances as it does the quality of our spiritual characters. God can test our eternal trust by observing our temporal trust. It's difficult to believe that even though we can trust God to deliver us from eternal death, we're somehow unable to believe God can be trusted to get us out of debt.

Certainly, God has not promised all believers personal wealth or what the world considers a high standard of living. But when we learn to give generously, we discover God is always capable of giving back more than we gave to start with.

True giving also involves a level of trust that comes when we don't seek to control every aspect of the gift. As we have seen, Malachi admonished the people to give to their spiritual "storehouse" (Malachi 3:10). People should give first and foremost to their local church, not only because of the practical needs of the church's ministry but because real giving means you don't control all uses of the money.

> We give out of our understanding that God is the source of all we have rather than giving because it makes sense financially.

Testimonies of Trust

God wants to bless us and demonstrate to the world that he will provide for our needs. Some of the greatest stories of American wealth are about the generosity of individuals.

William Colgate, the founder of Colgate-Palmolive Company, was an extraordinarily generous man whose goal was to give more than to earn. As his business prospered, his giving not only increased in amount but also in proportion.

James Cash Penney, who launched the J. C. Penney retail empire, gave away millions of dollars before the Great Depression. When the collapse of the economy during the depression caused him to lose most of what he had built, a newspaper reporter asked him, "Mr. Penney, do you regret all those millions you gave away to charity now that you are virtually broke and have to start over?" Penney replied, "My only regret was that I didn't give away more. The things I gave I still have in the way of hospitals, churches, and orphanages. It's the things I kept that were lost forever."

I've observed that some people resent the giving and receiving of personal wealth. But it also has been my careful observation that people tend to think of others as they think of themselves. The liar, for example, believes all people are liars and thus finds it difficult to accept the truth from anyone. The thief believes all others are stealing as well. It's only a matter of who will be caught and who will get away with it.

The person who is selfish believes all other people are selfish and thus is suspicious of those who are generous, believing they must have an ulterior motive. Such a person cannot accept the fact that some people are generous because of the joy they receive from giving things away. But this principle makes perfect sense to a person with a generous heart. That person gives not in hopes of getting something in return but merely to be like God.

The Ever-Expanding Circle of Generosity

Public officials are confronted with rules on the giving and receiving of gifts. I think it's a good idea to disclose to the public the types and scope of gifts. Voters should be able to evaluate the relationships that those in public office have and decide whether the givers are exerting too much influence.

But the trend in many states is to regulate and even prohibit normal giving and receiving among friends and relatives. These rules often are made by those who don't understand that true giving is not about seeking to influence someone. In the true spirit of giving, the person who received a gift is not so much obligated to return the favor as he is to pass on a similar blessing to another. Thus, this transaction becomes an ever-expanding circle of compassion and generosity.

If money means a great deal to us, then we will resent being asked to give it away. And we'll resent it when other people give because this reveals our lack of generous hearts. Since we're all going to leave this life as empty-handed as we were when we entered, learning to give things away develops God's generous spirit as part of our characters. It also means practicing letting go of the things we will ultimately let go of anyway.

The slogan of the 1992 presidential campaign—"It's the economy, stupid"—seems a little on the crude side. So maybe a kinder way to say it is this: "It's the money, honey."

QUESTIONS FOR REFLECTION AND DISCUSSION

1. How does the author define *stewardship?* Do you agree or disagree with his definition? Why?

2. In your opinion, what does it mean to be a "cheerful" giver?

3. Why do you think people are sensitive about the topic of giving and receiving money?

4. How is it possible for people to "rob" God, since he is the ultimate owner of the world and everything in it?

5. Do you think God's command of the tithe still applies to modern believers? Why or why not?

15

USING WHAT
YOU HAVE

THE RUNAWAY SUCCESS of the television game show *Who Wants to Be a Millionaire?* was a cultural phenomenon. Sociologists are trying to determine exactly what drove huge audiences to a simple game show in which contestants had to answer increasingly difficult questions in an attempt to win one million dollars.

There's perhaps something in all of us that asks, "What would I do with a million dollars?" While most of us are quite confident of what we would do with the money, the bigger challenge in life is doing something responsible with what we do have.

Many of us believe our lives would be far more successful if we could change things that are beyond our power to change. We think things like, *If I were a foot taller, I might be able to play in the NBA.*

If I were more attractive, I might land a movie role. If I had a lot of money, I would donate significant amounts to charity and make it possible for children to have lifesaving operations.

The God who placed us on this earth has a detailed inventory of our personal resources. It's much more appealing to fantasize about what we would do with imaginary treasures than it is to be faithful with the riches we actually possess. Yet using what we have, rather than what we wish we had, is especially important in three areas of life.

Use What's in Your Head

When Jesus fed five thousand people with a boy's lunch, he did so by taking what was available and believing that with God's strength it would be adequate (Mark 6:30–44). At first, the disciples who were with Jesus saw only a need and couldn't imagine any resource to meet it. This was true, although they had seen their Master speak to a storm and calm it and had seen him heal the critically ill.

The disciples had even seen Jesus take something as simple as water and turn it into the finest wine. They lived with a type of "spiritual amnesia." They were having a difficult time recalling the miracles they had witnessed and thus were limiting their options to what they knew within themselves.

Many of us are tempted to assume that what we have will not make much difference in the world. We do, in fact, possess the power to leave our footprints in the world in a powerful way. We perhaps have said to someone, "I would never make it through the pain of that kind of surgery," although we later did just that. Just when we wonder how we might handle the loss of a job, we end up actually losing our job and find out things about ourselves that we never knew.

In her autobiography *The Hiding Place*, Christian author and Holocaust survivor Corrie ten Boom told about when she would take childhood train trips with her father. During a particularly anxious moment in Corrie's life, her father calmed her by asking, "Corrie, when you and I go to Amsterdam—when do I give you your ticket?" She replied, "Why, just before we get on the train." Her father said, "Exactly. And our wise Father in heaven knows when we're going to need things, too. Don't run out ahead of Him, Corrie."[1]

God doesn't give us grace for the experiences we don't face—only for the experiences we do face. He never fails to equip us for the experiences we have.

We will usually not be adequately equipped for a task solely in our capacity at the moment. We must know God will supply the energy we need to survive and succeed.

Use What's in Your Hand

When Jesus fed the multitudes, he did not ask the location of the nearest grocery store. Instead, he asked the disciples, "How many loaves do you have?" (Mark 6:38). As the disciples surveyed their inventory, all they could come up with was the equivalent of five biscuits and a couple of small fish. By the biblical description, that's the lunch of a little boy, hardly enough for an adult and woefully inadequate to feed thousands of people.

The disciples began to argue among themselves because they could focus only on what they had. And in their minds, that was inadequate. But Jesus took a boy's small lunch and transformed it into enough food to feed the multitudes.

We are not called to be successful as much as we're called to be faithful. In the great scheme of things, it's faithfulness that makes us successful rather than the other way around.

A life done well is not so much the result of great achievements as it is our faithfulness. When we have faith, we can be reminded of how God has taken care of us thus far, take an inventory of our present resources, and believe that God will enable us to be adequate as we carry out his directions in the future.

Use What's in Your Heart

When Jesus took the small amount of food and thanked God for it, it was exactly the opposite of what most of us do when confronted with inadequate resources for the tasks we face. Jesus thanked God for what we would have complained about. We often find ourselves making speeches to God about the inadequacy of what we have rather than thanking him for stretching our possessions until our needs are met.

The miracle Jesus performed in feeding thousands of people revealed to the disciples that what appears to be insufficient is more than capable of meeting whatever needs exist. Not only did Jesus thank God for the little that was there, but he also ordered that the food be distributed. On the surface, it would appear that when a person has little, it's best to hold on to it. But as we saw in the previous chapter, giving releases the power for a little to become a lot.

It's easy to imagine the influence we might have if only we were blessed with greater strength, wealth, or health. The energy we use imagining what *could be* often robs us of what *should be*.

Several years ago, it was my pleasure to know a man named Bill Garner. He was a member of my church in Pine Bluff, Arkansas. Bill was in his seventies. Severe diabetes had left him blind and barely able to get around on the artificial legs he had as the result of amputations. If anyone had a reason for saying, "I don't have much to offer," it was Bill. No one would have thought of Bill as shirking his responsibilities if he had pointed to his lack of eyesight and mobility and excused himself from any meaningful service.

But Bill Garner would hear nothing of it. Perhaps he couldn't walk door to door, make lengthy speeches, or play on the church softball team, but Bill could dial the phone. Every week, he made more than one hundred calls to encourage people who were sick and to invite others to church. A telephone might not seem like much, but it became a powerful tool in Bill Garner's hand.

Robert Tollison was a young deacon at Immanuel Baptist Church in Pine Bluff. During the week, he worked in the parts department of a heating and air conditioning company. He worked long hours, but he didn't have the kind of job that made him rich. When Robert reached into his pockets, there wasn't a great deal of money. But Robert could pull out a large set of keys. Each Sunday,

> We are not called to be successful as much as we're called to be faithful. In the great scheme of things, it's faithfulness that makes us successful rather than the other way around.

Robert arrived early to unlock the many doors at the church. He then spent time making sure the temperature was comfortable in all parts of the facility. Robert would come in the night before a baptism, fill the baptistery, and make sure the water was warm.

Robert never received a standing ovation for his efforts. Few would have known to express their thanks to him for arriving at the church hours before them and staying after they left so the pastor and the church staff could spend more time being attuned to the spiritual needs of the congregation. Robert took what he had—a set of keys and a knowledge of heating and cooling systems—and did a service for people who probably never recognized it.

Pam Burns, a young wife and a mother of two, was a member of Beech Street First Baptist Church in Texarkana, Arkansas. She was faithful in her attendance. Pam was not the type who drew attention to herself. I don't recall that she ever sang in the choir or stood to be heard during a church business meeting. But she had a very special gift of calligraphy.

During my first political campaign in 1992, the mail would bring a simple white postcard with an encouraging verse of Scripture. Those cards would arrive every day. Each of them was mailed anonymously. The daily Scripture verse became so meaningful and the faithfulness of its delivery so predictable that my wife and I would find ourselves racing to the mailbox to see what word of encouragement awaited us.

It wasn't until months after the campaign had ended that we discovered our secret prayer partner was Pam. Her faithful expressions of encouragement brought more hope and strength to us than she ever could have known, and we will forever be grateful.

Katy Elkins was a college librarian who somehow found time to clip every newspaper article she could find about my first political campaign. She compiled several large scrapbooks that we will always cherish. It's impossible to estimate the number of hours Katy spent gathering, sorting, and pasting the thousands of clips and other items in those scrapbooks. The scrapbooks will not be turned into bestsellers, but they hold a priceless value for us.

Frank and Katie Stone are a retired couple whom I came to know at Immanuel Baptist Church in Pine Bluff. Frank wasn't one who liked to speak in front of an audience or even lead in prayer, but he and Katie were excellent cooks. Whenever someone in the church experienced a difficult time such as a death or a serious illness in the family, a meal would appear at their home. Others could be called on to lead in prayer or give speeches. That was fine, because Frank and Katie could always be found in the kitchen making something delicious.

What's in your hand? It may be something as simple as a telephone, a set of keys, a ballpoint pen, a bottle of glue, or a cooking utensil. When each of us uses what we have and does it in such a way that other people's lives are touched, it will have a far greater impact than if we had written them a check for one million dollars.

I've known people who have had millions of dollars, and it made them no happier. In some cases, they wasted it and had nothing to show except expensive appliances that eventually broke, cars that had to be replaced, clothes that went out of style, and large homes that were without love and friendship. But for as long as I live and into the next life, I'll be grateful for those people who shared their talents and did it in such extraordinary ways.

QUESTIONS FOR REFLECTION AND DISCUSSION

1. What do you think the author means when he says the disciples of Jesus had a type of "spiritual amnesia"?

2. Do you believe that God equips believers for the experiences they face in life, no matter how difficult they may be? Why or why not?

3. The author gives several examples of people who used their gifts and talents for God's glory. Do you know someone whom you could add to this list of those who effectively used their gifts? Take time to thank God for these people and their influence in your life.

4. In what ways has God taken inadequate resources, such as he did with the boy's lunch in feeding the multitudes, and worked a miracle in your own life?

5. Do you agree with this statement by the author: "We are not called to be successful as much as we're called to be faithful"? Why or why not?

16

NO PAIN, NO GAIN

THE CHIPPER, YOUNG PHYSICAL THERAPIST exclaimed, "No pain, no gain!" She was putting my right leg through a series of contortions to help my knee recover from surgery after an automobile accident.

I was simply trying to help her in making some "gain." For some reason, she seemed to think I would be greatly encouraged every time she put my leg through a movement that caused a primal scream. On several occasions when she grabbed my leg, hoisted it into the air, and told me, "Lift it this way!" I responded, "If I could lift my leg that way, I wouldn't need physical therapy."

I finally was released from physical therapy, but I will always remember her motto: "No pain, no gain."

There's simply no painless way to live a life done well. Let's face it: some things in life aren't pleasant. Even a hard-core optimist would struggle to find something pleasant in circumstances such as the death of a child, the loss of a good job, or the sudden failure of a marriage. Some of the most important parts of our personal characters are forged during our times in the furnace of trials, when impurities are burned away. We are shaped by life's hurts. They help us understand the difference between our pleasures and our treasures.

Good from Bad

One of the most misquoted verses in the Bible is Romans 8:28: "And we know that in all things God works for the good of those who love him, who have been called according to his purpose."

Let's be clear—the Bible never says, "All things are good." Frankly, some things are bad. When a drunk driver crosses the centerline, runs into an oncoming car, and kills a family, that's not good. When a thirty-three-year-old mother of two young children dies of breast cancer, that's not good. When a faithful husband discovers his wife is cheating on him, that's not good.

I will never forget one particular tragedy that was a stark reminder that not all things are good in this world. Just before Thanksgiving in 1984, I was asked to come to the local funeral home to bring comfort to a grieving family. At the time, I was serving as pastor of Immanuel Baptist Church in Pine Bluff, Arkansas, but no amount of seminary training could have prepared me for what was ahead.

One day earlier, a young father in the process of a contentious divorce had picked up his two children, ages five and three, for what

NO PAIN, NO GAIN

was to have been a trip to Walmart to buy them a toy. The family was poor, so poor it had delayed the inevitable divorce. The mother kissed each of the children. They were filled with anticipation that the trip would yield a new toy as they spent time with a father they weren't seeing much anymore.

After three or four hours, the mother became worried because they had not returned. She called the sheriff's office, and deputies started to search for the missing children. A deputy spotted a car parked off highway US 270 between Pine Bluff and Sheridan, Arkansas, almost invisible from the road. The vehicle fit the description of the car in which the children had last been seen. The officer parked his cruiser and began searching the woods just beyond the car.

In a small clearing less than fifty yards from the edge of the highway, this veteran law enforcement officer saw something that would forever mark the lives of all who would become involved in this situation. The father never took the children to Walmart. He had previously purchased two nylon ski ropes and tied them together. He made slip knots that formed nooses and then tied the other end of the ropes to a limb a few feet above the ground. With a child in each arm, he had climbed a crudely constructed ladder and placed the nooses around the necks of the children and then himself. He jumped, killing himself and the two innocent children.

Some of the most important parts of our personal characters are forged during our times in the furnace of trials, when impurities are burned away.

At the time, two of my children were almost the same ages as the children who had been murdered. As I escorted the mother to see her children's bodies in their caskets, I was struck as to how unnatural the scene was. Here were what appeared to be sleeping children with pudgy hands folded over, children who in their final moments on this earth must have asked, "Daddy, why are we here? Daddy, what is that rope for? Daddy, I don't want to get on that ladder. Daddy, this rope scratches my neck." Compounding the horror was the report from the coroner, who indicated the children had struggled to free themselves.

After the funeral service, Adam Robinson Jr., the funeral director with whom I had ridden to the cemetery, asked if I would like to stop for a cup of coffee. In the dozens of funeral services we had conducted together, we had never before made a stop on the way back. But today was different. I was glad he had mentioned it. I was no more ready to go back and face the normal routine than he was. We both needed some time for emotional reentry into a world that seemed cold and heartless.

It was the middle of the afternoon. We sat for an hour or so with very little conversation. We were oblivious to other customers in the small café and hardly aware of the coffee cups we held. Adam and I were close to the same age. We both had small children at home. Our children spent a little more time in our laps that evening and were hugged a little tighter.

Experiences like that are harsh reminders that some things in life are anything but good. But those who love God need not stretch their faith to validate Romans 8:28. The Bible doesn't say all things are good. The Bible does say that "in all things God works

142

for the good." But even then, we must note that things only work together for the good of "those who love [God], who have been called according to his purpose."

Working Together for Good

How can all things work together for good when so many things oppose the good? Let me try to explain.

When my wife, Janet, and I moved to Fort Worth, Texas, for me to attend graduate school in January 1976, we struggled financially as most young couples do in similar circumstances. Our struggle intensified when Janet became pregnant. We lost her income but gained the expenses of a baby. We had to make do on the little bit of money I earned. For almost six months, our daily meals consisted of peanut-butter-and-jelly sandwiches and alternating flavors of canned soup.

On the advice of one of our friends, Janet enrolled in a cake decorating course at a nearby department store with the hope she could decorate cakes to earn a little extra money. Before she could actually make the cakes, she had to invest in several pans and the "squeeze bags" through which the frosting would be applied to the cakes. (A word of advice to husbands: If your wife tells you she's going to decorate cakes to earn some extra income, do yourself a favor and don't let it happen.) Though Janet turned out to be an impressive cake decorator, we nearly went broke "making extra money." After working hard on an elaborate cake, she announced to me, "This is for Glenda's birthday. Since we can't afford to get her a present, I'm going to let the cake be my gift." I knew of the hours of work that had gone into decorating a cake. I would ask Janet how much she received for a particular cake. Usually I was greeted with the news that the cake was for one of our friends, so she didn't feel comfortable charging for it.

I did learn a lot about decorating cakes, though. Janet's first step would be gathering the ingredients and arranging them on the kitchen counter. She then would measure, mix, and bake. I would sometimes come in from work and realize she would be unable to prepare dinner for me that evening. Being the considerate husband I was (and hopefully still am!), I would tell her not to worry about dinner. I then would proceed around the kitchen counter and begin to snack on the various ingredients. Sometimes I would take a large kitchen spoon, dip it into a can of Crisco, and eat directly from the can of shortening. I would follow that up by munching on a stick of butter or eating dry cocoa from a box. Those items would then be washed down by drinking from a bottle of vanilla extract. I would sometimes even eat a couple of cups of raw sifted flour. That way, I didn't have to wait for the cake.

Actually, I really didn't eat shortening from the can, butter, dry cocoa, flour, or any of the other ingredients. (I bet you were groaning as you read the paragraph above!) The individual ingredients of a cake aren't very appealing if eaten by themselves in their raw state. But we don't eat a cake by taking the ingredients one by one. The ingredients are measured and brought together using a carefully tested plan called a recipe. They're mixed and then subjected to an extraordinary fit of violence in a device called a mixer. In fact, rather violent words are used to describe its functions—words like *whip* and *beat*. After the ingredients have been put through the mixer, the violence intensifies. The freshly mixed ingredients, which now are unrecognizable from their original condition, are stuffed into an oven hot enough to make your blood boil. While in the oven, the structure changes from a goo to a spongy mass. Then—and only then—is the cake frosted and served for those who want the reward of something sweet and attractive.

Think about it: not one ingredient that goes into a cake is necessarily desirable by itself. We would not eat raw flour, dry cocoa, or shortening. The cake isn't judged by the individual ingredients but by how they taste after following the recipe. Then and only then should we assess the finished product.

Not every ingredient of life is pleasant. But when mixed with the other ingredients and subjected to various trials, they have the capacity to form lives that are ever closer to the character of Christ. As we attempt to live a life done well, we need to recognize that some elements of our lives will be unpleasant. But individual components working together with the other components can result in something good.

Responding to Pain

The pain in our lives is temporary. It will end when our lives end. Suffering is inevitable for human beings. It is not the presence of suffering but our response to it that determines whether we're made better or made bitter.

In the Sermon on the Mount, Jesus reminded us that our pain can drive us to a level of godliness we never would have known otherwise.

Blessed are the poor in spirit,
> for theirs is the kingdom of heaven.

Blessed are those who mourn,
> for they will be comforted.

Blessed are the meek,
> for they will inherit the earth.

Blessed are those who hunger and thirst for righteousness,
> for they will be filled. (Matthew 5:3–6)

At first it would appear to be a contradiction for Jesus to tell us we're happy when we're spiritually drained, when we experience a great loss, when we've had our will broken, or when we stand with deep hunger for what is right. But Jesus understood what most Americans don't understand in our quest for pain-free living. If we experience momentary suffering that makes us more like Christ and less like our selfish selves, then we are further along on the road to lasting joy.

Second Corinthians 4:17 is one of the most challenging verses of the Bible for me. In this verse, the apostle Paul wrote, "For our light and momentary troubles are achieving for us an eternal glory that far outweighs them all."

When I developed a kidney stone during a trip to Puerto Rico in 1998, I had to be temporarily hospitalized in a facility where virtually no one spoke English. I then had to be flown home for the removal of the kidney stone. It's hard for me to believe the apostle Paul could have been so callous as to call my experience "light and momentary"! (I am convinced the apostle Paul had never had a kidney stone. Had he experienced it, surely he would have written about an exception in describing human suffering as light and momentary.)

During that episode, I was probably as close to God as I've ever been. I was really praying to get even closer. I wanted to experience a medical miracle or go on to glory—which at the moment would have been fine with me. In my experience, the only thing worse than having a kidney stone is having a kidney stone while being governor. A detailed description of how it was removed was on the front page of the state's newspapers the next morning.

In the midst of our suffering, it's difficult to believe there's anything "light and momentary" about it. But from the

> But from the perspective of the eternal joy provided by a faith rooted in God's promises, even the worst earthly troubles are indeed minor and temporary.

perspective of the eternal joy provided by a faith rooted in God's promises, even the worst earthly troubles are indeed minor and temporary.

Some of life's circumstances help bring our stubborn human will under control. They force us to recognize our human weaknesses and vulnerability. Such experiences form the essence of the idea of "blessed are the meek."

Our Strength Under God's Control

When domesticating a wild animal, you must harness the raw power and make sure it will follow directions. Similarly, when our strength is brought under God's control, it doesn't mean we're weak. The Bible never says, "Blessed are the weak." There's a dramatic difference between meekness and weakness. Weakness means we've lost our strength. Being meek means we have learned how to have it under control and can channel it toward achieving useful goals.

Pain has a way of taming us. Pain can force us to be emptied of our pride and our sense of self-sufficiency. It makes us realize we can go from full speed to a dead stop in an instant. I don't like pain. I'm not at the point in my life where I welcome it, readily accept it, or consider it my friend. In the midst of a difficult moment, in fact, I may forget everything I'm saying in this chapter. But deep within me is the comforting truth that pain has a purpose. Because of my relationship with Jesus Christ, I can and will endure. Deep down, I realize that unpleasant experiences—no matter how unwelcome— will work with other experiences to bring about a deeper character and a greater sense of compassion for those around me who hurt in even greater ways. These experiences will make me grateful that my life on earth is not the only one I'm going to live.

Without a doubt, the greatest purpose of pain is to point me toward my eternal life in heaven. As I seek to find comforting words to offer a friend whose daughter was murdered, or as I awkwardly try to find a way to encourage a friend whose wife is dying of cancer, I find comfort in knowing that no matter how bad this occasion may be, God will "work for the good," though it may be in the next life before I fully understand how.

I pity those who think life consists of nothing more than their years on earth. The most tragic are those who believe their value as a human being is tied to their net worth and whose self-esteem is linked to how many people know them and like them. It's far better to have confidence that no matter how many life experiences come your way that can be characterized as bad, they're only small distractions and diversions as we journey toward a life beyond this one. The Bible tells us that it will be a life in which there will be no tears, no sorrow, no pain, no disease, and no death (Revelation 21:4).

We must accept the fact that life isn't always a party with chips and cheese dip—sometimes, life hurts. Really hurts. But as the physical therapist reminded me, "No pain, no gain."

QUESTIONS FOR REFLECTION AND DISCUSSION

1. Why do you think the author considers Romans 8:28 one of the most misquoted verses in the Bible?

2. Describe a bad event in your life through which God eventually worked things for good.

3. Identify a sorrow in your life today. Then ask yourself, "Is God using this bad thing to help me become a better person?"

4. Why do you think the apostle Paul considered his sufferings "light and momentary"?

5. Reflect on Jesus's words: "Blessed are the meek." Then ask yourself, "Am I allowing God's discipline to bring my strength under his control?"

Part Four

A LEGACY LOVED

17

HOW MUCH
WILL YOU
LEAVE BEHIND?

ONCE THERE WAS A MAN hunting in thick woods. He became tired because he had been walking all day. As he started home, it began to rain. Soon he was cold and wet. Then he came upon a cabin in the woods. There was no one in the cabin, but there was plenty of dry wood on the front porch.

The hunter took some wood and built a fire in the fireplace. The fire burned brightly, and the hunter was soon comfortable. He noticed a sign above the fireplace that read, "Friend, enjoy the comfort of this little cabin. Rest all you want and stay as long as you like. The only cost to you is to leave the woodpile a little higher than when you found it."

Billy Graham once said, "I've never seen a hearse pulling a U-Haul." Perhaps you have heard the story about the funeral of John D. Rockefeller. A bystander edged up to an accountant for Mr. Rockefeller and asked, "Say, just how much did he leave behind?" The accountant replied, "He left it all. He didn't take a thing with him."

Our Age of Consumerism

We live in an age of consumerism. Many people judge their worth not by how much they've earned but by how much they've spent. One of our state's economic forecasters reported regularly to me on the status of the Arkansas economy during my time as governor. I often heard about consumer confidence levels. This is viewed as an important barometer of the economy's strength.

On more than one occasion, it has occurred to me that many people have built their lives around the strength of their personal buying power. Their lives are based not only on their ability to buy things but on the things they buy. That is tragic.

At the height of the Texas oil boom, a successful oil millionaire decreed that he be buried in his custom Cadillac. An unusually large grave was dug, and the millionaire was propped in the driver's seat. As the car was being lowered into the ground, someone was heard to exclaim, "Man, that's living." Actually, that is not living at all. It is dying. The most expensive casket will not make up for a life that has been lived in spiritual poverty.

Driving down the highway one day, I was startled by a bumper sticker that proclaimed, "He who dies with the most toys wins." It is a sad value system that rates a person's worth by the accumulation of things that can wear out, rot, go out of style, or be stolen.

Some people preach that having much is a sin, but that is not what the Bible teaches. The issue of wealth is not how much you have but how you got it and what you do with it. The two basic commands regarding accumulating wealth contain a negative and a positive. The negative is not to "store up for yourselves treasures on earth" (Matthew 6:19). The positive is to "store up for yourselves treasures in heaven" (v. 20). Too many people judge the wealth of others by the property they own or the lifestyle they enjoy.

> The most expensive casket will not make up for a life that has been lived in spiritual poverty.

One of the greatest challenges of life is determining that our pleasure shouldn't be based on our treasure. When our enjoyment of life is defined by what we have accumulated, we're to be pitied rather than envied. Our treasure should never become our job, home, car, property, or any other "toys." Consumerism can be intoxicating and addictive. Those who are swept up in its power find occasional moments of ecstasy tied to the purchase of something. But as soon as the pleasure of the purchase subsides, they're already seeking another value-oriented high.

A young couple from Little Rock announced they were leaving a relatively comfortable upper-middle-class life to become missionaries in Indonesia. They said, "We've fulfilled the American dream, but it didn't fulfill us." Like the heroin addict who is never quite satisfied, a person who gets a rush from the sound of a cash register as it rings up another purchase is one who will never know the simple joy of contentment.

A sense of real peace is achieved only when you can say that material things are genuinely immaterial. It's not so much what we have but what has us that will determine our inner tranquility. Some people have a great deal but are not the least bit enamored by it. Others have precious little but are totally consumed with the obsession to have more. There's no prohibition in God's Word to having much, but there's a strong admonition not to allow even a little to possess us (Matthew 19:22–24).

Some people will end up prosperous even though it was not their goal to lay up great treasures on this earth. It just seems to happen naturally for them. That is not necessarily bad as long as they are responsible stewards of their wealth and share it generously.

None of us really owns anything. We may possess things, but when we die, they will be in the hands of someone else. Ultimately, God owns everything. Our role on this earth is primarily that of a caretaker—or to use the biblical expression, a steward.

If we use what we have for God's glory rather than our own, then we most likely are storing up heavenly treasures rather than earthly treasures. Our priority should always be the ultimate result rather than the immediate result. There's a marked difference between spending and investment. That which has lasting value—especially that which has the ability to bring spiritual blessings—is worth far more than those things that depreciate from the moment we buy them until they are thrown away.

A Priceless Legacy

A good barometer of the value of our possessions is to ask whether anyone will benefit from our wealth a century from now. If a parent gives a son a new car and fine clothes but fails to give him character, will the son have benefited in the long term?

My own parents never knew earthly wealth. Both grew up poor and were precluded from anything more than a high school education because of World War II and the necessity of supporting their family. By most earthly standards, their accumulations were meager. But what they did have was paid for in full and earned by the sweat of their brows.

On December 31, 1991, I announced to my congregation at Beech Street First Baptist Church in Texarkana, Arkansas, that I would resign as pastor in order to seek public office. I had told my parents of my intentions. My mother wrote me a letter dated December 30, 1991. Five days after writing the letter, she suffered a ruptured aneurysm in her brain. She lived until September 30, 1999, but she was never the same mentally or physically.

Her letter to me was read at her funeral. It is a precious reminder of what real treasure is all about. Her letter indicates that my inheritance is far more valuable than it would have been if she had left me a portfolio worth millions of dollars.

Dear Mike,

We realize that we do not have a gift with words or the gift of saying the right thing at the right time, but we do want to say a few words at this time. Of course, you realize that this is your earthly mother and father speaking and not your heavenly Father speaking.

When you were given to us by our heavenly Father, we certainly were not acquainted with God's Holy Spirit, so we tried the best we knew how to bring you and Pat up to do what was right, to know when things were right and to know when they were wrong, to do unto others as you would have them do unto you, be humble in all that you do and to say please and thank you, yes sir, yes ma'am, no sir, no ma'am, speak to everyone, call them by name, respect other people, and do what you could for those less fortunate than yourself.

We are so very very thankful to God for what you both have turned out to be, and we always thank God in our prayers for this.

Now that you both are grown up, married, and are parents yourselves, we have tried hard not to tell you what to do with yourselves, etc. (even though it is hard sometimes), and it is because of this that we have not interfered with any of your decisions. Instead we will swallow real hard and pray very much that God will help you both in everything you do.

To make a long story a little shorter, we love you both so very much, ask for your forgiveness wherein we have failed you, and shall continue to pray that you both will always seek and do God's will.

With much love,

Mom

Jesus reminds us we can only have one master. He said, "You cannot serve both God and money" (Luke 16:13). We will either serve the spiritual or the temporal. As inhabitants of planet Earth, we are involved in the world and its possessions. But we don't have to be obsessed with those possessions. After all, as the old gospel song says, "This world is not my home, I'm just a-passing through." One of the challenges of life is to determine whether our responsibilities to God are more important than fulfilling our desires.

What Are You Sending On Ahead?

A little boy was given two quarters. His father told him that one quarter was to be placed in the offering plate at church, and the other was for ice cream. As he walked along holding the quarters, he dropped one. As it rolled away, the little boy said, "Sorry, God, there went your quarter."

As I mentioned in a previous chapter, I once worked for James Robison, whose world outreach has spanned decades through evangelism, encouragement, and feeding hungry children. James once received a letter from a father in Arkansas following an outdoor crusade in that area. In the letter, the father related how his daughter had started attending church at age six because the church had a bus route near their home. The little girl begged her daddy each Sunday to go to church with her, but he would tell her he was too busy running his gas station. He said he had to work on Sunday to make sure they had plenty of money.

For several years the little girl faithfully attended church and urged her father to go with her. Each Sunday, he offered the same excuse. The girl finally stopped

> One of the challenges of life is to determine whether our responsibilities to God are more important than fulfilling our desires.

going to church. That provided a certain relief for the father, since he would no longer have to repeat his excuse.

A few years later, the man received a phone call and was summoned to the school his daughter attended. The daughter, now twelve years old, had been sitting in a car with several other students sniffing aerosol spray from a bag for the temporary high it gave them. That morning's high took her higher than she had ever been—to her death. An autopsy showed the girl was pregnant.

The final words of the father's letter were the most haunting: "James, please tell daddies not to live for material things while forgetting the spiritual."

It's certain that, someday, we will leave everything in this world behind. What is important is what we send on ahead.

QUESTIONS FOR REFLECTION AND DISCUSSION

1. What are the negative and positive commands that Jesus gave regarding the accumulation of wealth in Matthew 6:19–20?

2. Why do you think consumerism is intoxicating and addictive for some people?

3. What's the difference between owning things and letting the things we have own us?

4. Describe the specific values we should pass on to our children that are more important than a financial legacy.

5. How can a person store up "heavenly treasures" rather than "earthly treasures"? Which kind of treasures are you storing up right now?

18

THE FOLLOW FACTOR

I'M AN AVID DUCK HUNTER, and I come from a great place for it. Arkansas has some of the best duck hunting in North America. Some of my greatest days were those hunting alongside my Labrador retriever, Jet, who was my faithful companion for fifteen years before he went to chase ducks in the flooded timber of heaven.

Being in the great outdoors at sunrise and watching waterfowl answer the sound of the duck call is the second greatest part of the hunt. The greatest pleasure is watching a good dog retrieve. The third pleasure is the fellowship shared with others in the duck blind. As strange as it may seem to nonhunters, the least important aspect is pulling the trigger on the shotgun.

During duck season, I enjoy watching all kinds of waterfowl make their way down the Mississippi Flyway as they migrate from

Canada to Mexico. I've long been fascinated by the geese that fly in a V formation. Experiments in a wind tunnel have shown what happens in a V formation. Each goose creates an upward lift for the goose behind. The formation gives about 70 percent more flying range than if a goose flies alone. Researchers also discovered that when one of the geese gets behind, the others honk encouragement for it to keep up.

Like waterfowl that have an instinct to fly south in the winter, we have an intuition that causes us to look toward our future. We think in terms of what will be remembered of our lives and whether anything of significance will remain once we're gone.

The kind of leader we'll be is tied directly to what kind of follower we were for those who blazed the trail before us. We don't live in a vacuum. Someone is likely following in our footsteps in the same way we're following others.

Gaining Courage from Others

I've traveled to Israel many times during the past forty-five years, going several times a year. One of my favorite places is Masada, the ancient Roman fortress in the desert near the Dead Sea where about nine hundred men, women, and children took refuge and held off an entire Roman army for almost three years. The fall of Masada in AD 73 marked the end of a Jewish state until 1948, when Israel was reborn. The extraordinary history behind Masada and the captivating story of those final moments, when hundreds of Jews chose to die rather than subject themselves to Roman slavery, makes it one of the most interesting places in the world to visit.

My first trip to Masada in 1981 was one I'll long remember.

Prior to going, I had read all I could about it so I would be prepared for my pilgrimage to this special place. When we arrived at the flat-topped fortress in the desert, I saw a cable car that stretched from the base of the mountain to a landing area near the top of Masada. My heart sank. Since that time, I've overcome what was extreme acrophobia and now routinely ride in helicopters. I've even experienced a memorable ride in a hot-air balloon. On that first trip to Masada, though, my sense of adventure was far from developed.

The thought of getting into that cable car scared me. I tried to hide my fear, but sweat poured from my head, my hands were clammy, my heart was beating too fast, and my breath was shallow and rapid. Most people would have thought nothing of it. But for me, the thought of being suspended above nothing but rock was terrifying beyond description. I tried to talk my way out of the line.

> The kind of leader we'll be is tied directly to what kind of follower we were for those who blazed the trail before us.

As we approached the point of boarding the cable car, I was nearing nausea. Just then, I noticed a large group of Catholic nuns getting ready to board. There wasn't a hint of anxiety among them. In fact, they were laughing and acting as casually as if they were being seated for dinner. Perhaps it was my pride that took hold, but I thought, *If those Catholic sisters aren't afraid, then neither should I be.* I took a deep breath, boarded the cable car, and lived to tell about it. I've returned many times, and I've never again been afraid.

As I reflected on that experience and others like it, I was reminded that sometimes our desire to do something overwhelms our fear of doing it. One of the ways we challenge our fears is to recognize that others have taken similar steps and are alive and well.

Overcoming Our Fear of Death

It's natural to fear death. If we sat for long periods contemplating nothing but death, we would soon become neurotic. There's something disturbing about moving toward a destination we've never seen in order to spend eternity with many people we've never met.

Overcoming the fear of death involves recognizing we're not migrating alone. Like geese, we're part of a large family traveling in the same direction. One of the reasons the Bible commands us to meet together regularly (Hebrews 10:25) is so we can gain strength from those with whom we fly. They, in turn, can gain strength from us.

There's genuine efficiency achieved as we face our future with fellow travelers. When we're weary and lag behind, the encouragement of others becomes like the honking of the geese, cheering us on toward the next step, the next day, the next challenge.

We can face death more comfortably knowing that many people have gone before us. While we're not exactly sure what our journey will be like, we know it's a well-worn path. For Christian believers, we know that the one on whom our entire faith is focused has not only traveled through the valley of death but has returned to announce his victory over it.

We may have never passed this way before, but it doesn't mean the route is untested. Believing we will live beyond our lifetime is incredibly liberating. It translates into a zest for living and certain ambivalence about dying. Moving toward death isn't something any of us enjoys talking about. But for those who are confident that the destination is worth the process, it holds a certain sense of adventure.

I've spent countless hours flying in small airplanes, often in less-than-ideal weather. I've come to appreciate is the skill of a pilot who can successfully guide an aircraft through the most rugged conditions. One thing is for certain in such a situation: The pilot cannot act according to what he thinks or what he feels. He must fly the airplane by relying on instruments to tell him if he is up or down. He puts his complete trust in those instruments. Flight instructors often say, "A pilot who begins to trust his feelings rather than his instruments is already dead. What's left to be determined is the exact spot of the crash."

> Believing we will live beyond our lifetime is incredibly liberating. It translates into a zest for living and certain ambivalence about dying.

Keeping Our Eyes on God

The Old Testament tells that God's people spent forty years in the wilderness (Numbers 13–14). They were told to follow a pair of clouds and later the ark of the covenant. They didn't know where they were or where they were going, but they were instructed to keep their eyes fixed on the ark and follow by faith (Joshua 3:3).

One of the important lessons from this event is that God doesn't tell us to head out in the direction of our choice and do the best we can while he tags along to pick up the pieces. He goes ahead of us, inviting us to stay close and follow while ensuring us of a safe arrival. If we focus on the fact that we have not ventured through death's door, we'll be overwhelmed with the sense of dread. But if we keep our faith fixed on the God ahead of us who has traveled this way before, our steps will be firm, although we still might have moments of anxiety.

In the pilgrimage of our lives, it isn't necessary that we bring our plans to God for his approval. Our task is to accept and follow the plans he already has drawn out. A person who brings detailed plans to an architect, a recipe to a chef, or tools to a mechanic is one who already has rejected the expertise of the person he approaches. As we move toward the conclusion of our lives and the certainty of our deaths, we should not be so foolish as to tell God what it will be like. We must allow God to chart and steer our course.

Confidence from Those Who Made the Journey

In February 2000, I joined six governors at a meeting in Salt Lake City. We went to the Utah Olympic Park, site of the 2002 Winter Olympics. The governors were invited to take a crash course (no pun intended) in bobsled driving and then steer a bobsled down the Olympic course. Having grown up in Arkansas, I had never seen a bobsled, much less had the opportunity to drive one. Mental pictures of the bobsled under my command flying off the course and down a steep mountain had my stomach in knots.

I could barely sleep the night before. I woke up at 4:30 a.m., plugged my laptop computer into the hotel phone system, made an Internet connection (this was 2000, and ubiquitous Wi-Fi would be years away!), and spent two-and-a-half hours reading everything I could about bobsleds. I went into the experience with much greater knowledge but no less fear.

Once again, it was not a sudden surge of courage that caused me to get seated (awkwardly, I might add) in the bobsled and put my faith in the sixteen-year-old athlete who was my push-off man. It was the presence of dozens of television camera crews, newspaper photographers, and spectators. That's what caused me to consent to being pushed down an icy track carved along the mountainside, reaching speeds of more than sixty miles per hour, and experiencing four Gs of pull as we made the turns.

No, it was not courage. It was the fact that two governors already had made their bobsled trips before me. Word had filtered back that both had survived. And there were many people looking on. I knew that even if I was killed doing it, I would go out in a blaze of glory. If I backed out now, I would have a hard time facing my fellow governors again. The trip in the bobsled turned out to be the experience of a lifetime. It is one I'll forever cherish, though not likely repeat.

One day I will face death. I believe I'll pass through it successfully, not because I've overcome all my fears but because I'm confident of the God who has gone before me and made the journey successfully. And because I'm being cheered on toward the finish line by those around me.

QUESTIONS FOR REFLECTION AND DISCUSSION

1. The author describes how he overcame his acrophobia—extreme fear of heights. Is there some irrational fear in your own life? What do you need to do to overcome it?

2. What do you think the author means by this statement: "Overcoming the fear of death involves recognizing we're not migrating alone"?

3. In what ways has Jesus made it easier for his followers to face the inevitability of their own deaths?

4. God has not chosen to tell us everything we might like to know about death and the life beyond. Can you think of any possible reasons why he has not given us perfect knowledge about these matters?

5. What are some certainties that believers can count on as they think about death and the life beyond?

19

TOWARD
THE EXIT SIGN

"THERE ARE ONLY TWO CERTAINTIES IN LIFE—death and taxes." This statement is often repeated, but it is only half true, considering the number of people sent to jail for not paying their taxes. Not everyone pays taxes, but it's certain we will all die sooner or later, ready or not.

Some will leave this life rather naturally, much like those who shuffle toward the door at the end of the movie once the lights are turned on. Even though the seats are comfortable, there's really no reason to continue sitting there. Others may find the exit from this life to be like that of the person who wishes to go one way but is forced to go another by the overwhelming force of the crowd as it leaves the theater. Still others may leave long before the movie has ended. No matter how we go, death is certain.

Let's not be mistaken. Death is not our friend. It's a bitter enemy. Death takes a baby out of a mother's arms. It removes the voice of a father who speaks words of guidance and encouragement to his children. Death leaves an empty chair at the dinner table and stills the laughter at family gatherings. It causes people to regret the things they did and the things they failed to do as they stand over the coffin of a loved one.

The ways we deal with death have changed, even in my lifetime. I can remember the old Southern custom of "sitting up." Friends and relatives would take turns literally sitting with the body from the time of death until the time of burial. I can recall another tradition of having the body in the home rather than the funeral parlor. Years ago, it wasn't uncommon for people to go to the hospital to get well but come home to die.

The custom of "sitting up" is almost a thing of the past, and I don't recall a body being taken to a home in years. Frankly, I'm glad both of those traditions are in the rear-view mirror! Through organizations such as hospices, though, many people are returning to the idea that it's better to die in your home while comforted by family and friends. In the past several years, we've attempted to bring some dignity back to the process. It's hard to die with dignity in a hospital environment while surrounded by IVs, catheters, and respirators. There's the noise from the hospital corridors and the interruptions of the hospital staff being summoned to various locations. While customs may have changed, the fact that all of us will die has not changed.

Important Facts About Death

Most of us don't know the time, date, place, and circumstances of our death. It might happen suddenly with an accident or a heart attack. It might be a protracted process such as cancer. But there are some things we can and should know about death.

Death Is a Certainty for Everyone

The Bible teaches, "People are destined to die once, and after that to face judgment" (Hebrews 9:27). We live our lives as a series of appointments. My schedule is the most complicated aspect of my life. I am actually busier now than I've ever been. I was incredibly busy as governor, but I had several people working for me whose full-time jobs were to process the scheduling requests, evaluate them with various staff members, and then make the preparations for the events we did. And as governor, I only had one job. Now, I'm hosting a weekly television show on TBN (Trinity Broadcasting Network) from Nashville, working as a contributor for Fox News Channel, writing newsletters daily, leading groups to Israel and other parts of the world, delivering speeches all over the world, and dealing with several business interests. The travel is brutal. Some months I'm home no more than three nights in an entire month.

I'm amused when someone comes up to me and asks, "What are you doing on April 3?" Little do they know that I'm barely able to keep up with what I'll do tomorrow. But I've learned that the appointments on my calendar can be rescheduled when necessary. The important gives way to the urgent as every appointment is evaluated.

Most of us are used to rescheduling appointments, but the one appointment beyond rescheduling is our appointment with death. Death occurs to good people and bad people, to the faithful and the unfaithful. Death is inevitable whether we're rich or poor. Our religion may give us comfort as we approach death, but it will not change its inevitability. Death is the ultimate equalizer and the grim reminder that no matter how healthy, wealthy, or important we are, we're not invincible. We will die.

Death Is Determined by God

Jesus has the keys of life and death. Jesus said, "I am the Living One; I was dead, and now look, I am alive for ever and ever! And I hold the keys of death and Hades" (Revelation 1:18). Scripture also reminds us that we enter this life on our way out. Job 14:5 says, "A person's days are determined; you have decreed the number of his months and have set limits he cannot exceed."

All of us know people who should have lived but died. We also know people who should have died but lived. I remember being stunned by the death of fellow students when I was a teenager. Somehow it seemed impossible that someone my age could die. One classmate was recovering from a motorcycle accident with what seemed to be no more than a broken bone. A blood clot formed, dislodged, and killed him. It didn't seem real, but the grief of his family and friends was very real.

A high school classmate had barely started college when her date lost control of a car, slid off the road, and hit a tree. He walked away from the accident, but she was killed instantly. I'll never forget the funeral as hundreds of friends from high school and college tried to understand how a person so young, beautiful, and vibrant could be laughing and living one moment and be gone the next.

Now in my sixties, more often than I want to deal with, I learn of a classmate from high school or college passing away or someone I know from church or the community. It's a stark reminder that this life is fleeting. My wife and I often remind each other that we need to do some things we've been putting off because we never know when our health or circumstances will prohibit the items on our bucket list.

Technology has extended the lives of thousands who a few years ago would have died. But while the advancement of technology can change the outlook for the immediate, it cannot change the ultimate.

Death Leaves an Empty Space

When a person dies, we can do no more for that person or to that person. Yet many people desperately attempt to continue a relationship with a deceased loved one. In the Bible, even Saul tried to talk to the dead (1 Samuel 28:7–15). Many still do. Others simply deny the death of a loved one has occurred.

One of the most difficult parts of the grief process is to accept the reality of death and the transition from a time of mourning to a time of reentry into life. In 2 Samuel, we read about the extraordinary grief experienced by King David following the death of his son. But David was encouraged as he realized the time for mourning had ended and it was time to accept responsibility for the living (12:15–23).

After a death, there are many practical things that must be confronted. We must deal with funeral arrangements, disposing of the person's personal items, tying up loose ends, and going through what seems to be an endless pile of paperwork dealing with insurance, Social Security, and estate matters. As we move beyond the death of a relative or friend, the vacuum left by the death can create a great level of discomfort.

Some people's lives become empty after the death of a loved one, since their days had been filled with activities related to the deceased. The routine of caring for a person can become so ingrained that the caregiver doesn't realize how many hours each day he or she was spending on the task. The caregiver suddenly has a lot of time on his or her hands. The lack of something to do creates anxiety and sometimes even guilt.

One of the world's most comprehensive researchers on the subject of death is Dr. Elisabeth Kübler-Ross. In her classic work *On Death and Dying*, she describes the five stages of grief: denial, anger, bargaining, grieving, and acceptance.[1] Dr. Kübler-Ross found that though the stages may come in different degrees and in a different order for different people, each stage is part of the grief process.

At some point, we want to deny that a relative or friend is actually dying. There will be anger—perhaps at God, perhaps at medical personnel, or perhaps at the drunk driver whose actions killed our loved one. It's not unusual for a person to engage in a period of bargaining: "God, if you let my loved one live, then I'll be more faithful and will forgive all the people who have wronged me." Grieving grows out of the natural sense of sorrow and hurt.

Finally, although it may take years for some people, there's a sense of acceptance. That's not to say we're content with the death. Acceptance may not mean that things return to normal. It simply means we face the reality that our loved one isn't coming back and that we must go on with our lives.

Death Displays God's Judgment

Physical death is not always because of a specific sin for which God punishes us. But there's a sense in which all death is the result of the universal sin in our world and in our lives. If there had been no sin, there would be no death. But because there is universal sin on earth, there will be universal death. Some people believe each death is the direct result of God's getting angry or getting even with someone. This view is not only far from the biblical teaching, but it's just plain cruel. None of us can know for certain why another person died.

Perhaps the most insensitive thing I've ever seen was when a misguided friend said to the parents of a child who had just died, "You need to pray and find out what you did to make God take your child from you." Some deaths, according to Hebrews, occur because the deceased is simply too good to go on in this world (Hebrews 11:37–38). Death is, in fact, a reward for a life well lived.

During my time as a pastor in Pine Bluff, Arkansas, my children were very young. One Sunday night after church, a couple invited us to their home for refreshments. They were older and had not had children in their home for years.

On the way to their home, my wife and I instructed our three children, whose ages ranged from three to nine, to be on their best behavior. We told them not to touch anything or pick anything up. We further instructed them that they were to sit politely and behave. They weren't to eat or drink anything that could easily be spilled. Like little angels, each of them said they understood.

As we walked through the front door of the nicely appointed home, I was shocked to see that not only was the home decorated with delicate treasures on each shelf and table but that there also was lush white carpet. I suddenly instructed the children that they were not hungry or thirsty, their hands needed to remain in their pockets, and they were not to touch anything!

Somehow the halos on my children turned into horns. Soon, they were trotting off with the man and lady of the house, asking questions about the treasures on the shelves and occasionally picking up items. The problem was there were three of them and only two of us as parents.

Things got worse when the lady of the house announced she wanted to serve us hot fudge sundaes. The thought of my three children dropping hot fudge on that white carpet caused me to lose any desire for ice cream. One by one, I took my children down the hall to the restroom despite their loud insistence they didn't need to go. The purpose of the trip was to make sure they understood our agreement not to touch anything, eat anything, or drink anything.

I'm sure they meant well, but by the time they were back down the hall the promises were forgotten. The things on the shelves were too much to resist. So was the allure of ice cream dripping with hot fudge.

I was convinced my kids would not keep their promise of a hands-off policy, and there was no way our hosts' beautiful white carpet could be kept from having a coating of hot fudge. It was at that point I gave my wife something every couple understands. I gave her "the look."

You know what I mean. It's that unspoken communication that causes a mother to look at her watch, smile, and graciously say, "My, I didn't realize how late it is. As much as we would love to stay, we really need to get home and put the kids to bed. But we certainly enjoyed being here." We gathered the children up and left in order to spare ourselves embarrassment.

In some ways, there may be times when our heavenly Father takes someone home earlier than expected in order to protect his good name and to spare our earthly environment from any additional destructive behavior on that person's part.

Regardless of why a person dies, one thing is certain: Only God knows when the right time is. Even then, he does it for our good as well as his. It's certainly not something we should speculate about.

Death Is Different for Believers

During my tenure as a pastor, I officiated almost four hundred funerals. I have seen firsthand that while believers don't escape death, they do overcome it. One of the most powerful sermons I've heard regarding death and the preparation for it was titled "Born Once, Die Twice—Born Twice, Die Once." In other words, a person who is born but does not have faith in Jesus will not only die a physical death on earth but also experience spiritual death in eternity. But a person who is born and then born again through faith in Jesus will die only once on earth and then live forever in heaven.

The greatest hope we have as believers is that we have life that is eternal. Our faith as Christians is grounded in the belief that Jesus Christ not only died but rose from the grave.

We might say, "I'm going to fly to New York." We don't actually do the flying. The airplane does. But because we are in the airplane, we go wherever it goes. This is what it means to be "in Christ." It isn't that we have the power to overcome death and have everlasting life. But Jesus overcame death and has eternal life. If we are in him, then we share in his destination.

There's no greater hope in all the human heart than to know that the inevitability of death is met with the assurance that life doesn't end. The Bible makes clear that the life beyond death is one in which there are no headlines, no hospitals, no hurts, no hardships, no heat waves, no heart attacks, and no humiliations. There is no homelessness, no hunger, and no hell.

Not only is the destination decidedly different for believers, but the process of facing death is remarkably different for believers as well. The custom at most funerals is that after the memorial service, the family is given a few moments for one last viewing of the body before the trip to the cemetery. In the hundreds of funerals I conducted, I heard a kind of weeping in those families where faith abounded that was different from those families where faith was absent. In each case, the grief was real, and the tears were genuine. But those who had faith cried with a loss that sounded as if it at least had a bottom. Those who believed death ended all relationships and that nothing existed after this life cried with a haunting sense of emptiness and abandonment.

This type of weeping went beyond mere crying. It was what the

Scriptures describe as "weeping and gnashing of teeth" (Matthew 25:30). It was a gut-wrenching sense of grief that sounded as if it were coming from a pit without a floor. It was chilling to the bone.

Death Divides God's Treasures

The Bible teaches that we will be judged. As believers, we won't face a future judgment as to whether we will have eternal life. That is determined by our faith rather than our works. But neither heaven nor hell is a place of equals.

Revelation 20:12–13 says, "I saw the dead, great and small, standing before the throne, and books were opened. Another book was opened, which is the book of life. The dead were judged according to what they had done as recorded in the books. The sea gave up the dead that were in it, and death and Hades gave up the dead that were in them, and each person was judged according to what they had done."

Clearly, there are eternal rewards based on the manner in which we lived our lives on earth. In the same way, the Scriptures teach that hell is not the same, though it could be argued there's no part of it that could be comfortable enough to be called tolerable. It starts bad and only gets worse. Hell for child molesters and serial killers is most likely even more intense than for the person who out of sheer spiritual rebellion rejected God's hope.

Death Destroys Human Accomplishment

No matter what we've done and how well we've done it, it's certain that at the moment of our death, our independence comes to a halt. The great and mighty are equally as dead as the lowly and poor.

We come into the world without possessions, and we leave without possessions.

Many stores have installed devices so a person trying to exit with unpurchased merchandise triggers an alarm. Death is an even more effective alarm system. As we have seen, no matter what we have accumulated in this life, we will leave it at the door when we reach the exit. When we think about how temporary our possessions are, it makes the things we do to accumulate them seem silly and meaningless.

> No matter how much wealth and power we attain, those possessions and that power depart the moment we draw our final breath.

It's easy to envy those people who have nicer cars, expensive homes, more fashionable clothes, and the other trappings of worldly success. There's nothing wrong with possessing things, but there's something tragic about being possessed by those things. No matter how much wealth and power we attain, those possessions and that power depart the moment we draw our final breath.

We cannot stop the process of death. The best doctors and the best medicine can only slow it down. We can't prevent it, but we can prepare for it. In the gospel of John, Jesus tells us not to be troubled or afraid. He gives us a wonderful promise: "I go and prepare a place for you" (John 14:3).

QUESTIONS FOR REFLECTION AND DISCUSSION

1. Why do you think some people attempt to communicate with the dead?

2. Look back through the five stages of grief described in this chapter. Have you experienced these stages? Describe the process you went through.

3. Do you agree with this statement by the author: "There's a sense in which all death is the result of the universal sin in our world and in our lives"? Why or why not?

4. Have you ever known a person who refused to accept the fact that a loved one had died? What behavior did this person demonstrate?

5. What hope do Christians have that makes facing death different for them than it is for non-Christians?

20

THE LEGACY
OF YOUR LOOT

Most Americans will tell you money might not guarantee happiness, but it sure helps. Few subjects bring stronger reactions than the topic of money. Friendships are lost because of it. Marriages are destroyed because of it. Churches split over the spending of it. Political campaigns are fought over how it's received and spent.

One of the most commonly misinterpreted verses in the Bible is about money. Many people think the Bible says money is the root of all evil. The Bible never says money is the root of all evil. It says, "The love of money is a root of all kinds of evil" (1 Timothy 6:10). There are two kinds of people in the world: those who admit they are affected by money (or the lack thereof) and those who lie and say they're not affected.

How to Leave the Right Legacy with Your Loot

Not everyone has a love of money, but all of us need enough of it so we can feed our families, put gasoline in our cars, keep roofs over our heads, and have clothing on our backs. Some people who have a lot of wealth love money less than those who have little. Net worth is not an indication of a healthy relationship with personal wealth.

While the most important legacy we leave is our character, this chapter presents five basic principles of leaving the right kind of legacy with our loot.

Provide Honest Resources for Your Family

Since the time of Adam, hard work has been a spiritual as well as a practical requirement for honest wages. Proverbs 10:4 says, "Lazy hands make for poverty, but diligent hands bring wealth."

The rapid growth of various forms of gambling in our culture has fueled the notion that it's possible to get something for nothing. But wagering will never produce wealth in a manner as predictable as work. If the vice of making a bet was as valid as the virtue of getting a job, few people would invest their resources in the stock market or use their money to start companies. The truly wealthy people I know don't take their money to casinos or buy lottery tickets.

After growing tired of hearing an extremely wealthy man grumble, a man of modest means said, "I have very little. You have millions. But I'm richer than you because I have as much as I need or want. Sadly, you don't."

While we read of an occasional person who falls into money, most of us don't suddenly become rich. There are rare exceptions—

such as the couple whose sewer lines collapsed. As they dug, the man found a few gold coins and then some more. He ended up discovering coins worth more than $1 million. The coins were left over from the gold rush of 1849. The likelihood of that happening for most of us is about the same as winning a multimillion-dollar sweepstakes.

Perhaps you heard about the person who was excited when he was told he had just won three million dollars in a sweepstakes. He lost his enthusiasm when he was informed he would receive one dollar a year for the next three million years.

Pay Debt Promptly

The Bible speaks of debt as a trap and those who are taken captive by debt as slaves (Proverbs 6:1–5). Americans are certainly adept at borrowing money. I am reminded of the story of an immigrant who came to this country without a dime but in less than a year owed $400 million! Yes, Americans believe in borrowing.

Some Christians believe you should never borrow money under any circumstance. The Bible teaches that we should pay what we owe and not obligate ourselves for what we cannot pay. The prohibition is against failing to pay off debt and accumulating debts that are beyond our capacity to pay back in a reasonable amount of time. Few things hurt a person's testimony of faith more than being irresponsible with debts to others.

A scoundrel in the community became very religious. A friend said, "I hear you're starting to attend church. I guess that means you'll be giving up drinking, smoking, and cussing. Does that also mean you're going to be paying off your debts?" The newly converted scoundrel replied, "Wait a minute. That's not religion; that's business."

As difficult as it is to leave a positive legacy, it's not difficult to leave a negative legacy by failing to pay debts or, even worse, leaving your heirs with the burden of paying them. We certainly shouldn't be like the ambitious young man who ran up debts all over town. One of the merchants to whom he owed a considerable sum approached him one day and said, "Look, I've about had it waiting for you to pay me. I need my money this week." The young man replied, "Please don't talk to me so harshly. If you do, I'll take your name out of the hat." The merchant asked what he meant.

> As difficult as it is to leave a positive legacy, it's not difficult to leave a negative legacy by failing to pay debts or, even worse, leaving your heirs with the burden of paying them.

The young man said, "Each month, I take all the bills I receive and put them in a large hat. I draw from the hat and pay the bills until I run out of money. Then I put all the other bills in the hat and leave them there until the next month's drawing." When the merchant complained that such a procedure was unacceptable, the young man repeated, "If you're going to be that way about it, I'll quit putting your bills in the hat."

Plan Your Purchases Carefully

Another principle of sound financial management is to avoid impulse buying. Most of the time we buy things that have no lasting value. One of the challenges of being an American when the economy is good is to be honest with ourselves when it comes to buying what we need rather than what we want. We should be responsible stewards when it comes to managing what we have. We should do our best to shop for the best prices and wait for sales. This enables us to leave more for rainy days and to preserve a financial legacy for our children and grandchildren.

John Wanamaker, a successful businessman in the nineteenth century, bought his first Bible at age eleven. Later in life, he said, "I've made purchases involving millions of dollars, but the little Bible I bought for $2.75 was my best investment ever. It was the foundation of my life."

A life done well involves not only leaving things behind but also passing on a lifestyle that will allow our children to remain debt free.

Protect Your Assets Diligently

It's wrong for us to hoard things, but it's equally wrong to fail to protect our assets. Being able to take care of our possessions not only indicates our trust in God but also teaches our children how to manage money and material things.

A beggar approached a pedestrian and said, "Give me a dollar." The pedestrian replied, "I might give you a dime or a quarter, but I'm not giving you a dollar." The beggar said indignantly, "Hey, you can give me a dollar or not, but don't tell me how to run my business." Being a good manager of the resources God has entrusted us with involves insuring what we can't afford to replace. We should also make long-range financial plans and invest the money we don't need for current expenses for the future.

Practice Unselfish Giving Cheerfully

The subject of giving is one of the most often preached about but least often practiced.

As believers, we don't give to churches or ministries to bail "poor ol' God" out of trouble. The reason a person of faith gives isn't because the recipient has a need to receive but because the giver has a need to give. Only through giving do we learn to have an unselfish spirit. The people who are willing to end friendships over financial issues are the ones for whom money has become more important than God.

We shouldn't be concerned about how others make or spend their money as long as it is honest. But those whose hearts are greedy, whose spirits are selfish, and who covet what others have are quick to criticize and condemn others for what they possess, how they received it, and what they do with it. The quickest way to discover who has an unhealthy love for money is to talk about the good fortune of someone who came into an unexpected treasure. The person who expresses resentment about this is probably someone possessed by the love of money.

True believers realize that whatever money or material possessions we have are temporary. We are not so much enamored with God's gifts as we are enamored with the God who gave the gifts. The Bible admonishes us to honor God with the "firstfruits" of our lives (Exodus 34:26). This is a way to prove we trust him, not merely by saying the words but by living out the deeds.

The best kind of giving in the world is the giving that cannot be repaid. Giving to those who will give back isn't really giving; it's trading. True spiritual giving involves an extraordinary level of faith and is motivated by our character, not by our desire to receive a return favor for the gift.

A reporter traveling to write articles on mission work came upon a missionary who was treating the sores of lepers. The reporter said, "I wouldn't do that for a million dollars." The missionary replied, "Neither would I. But I'm more than happy to do it in service to my Savior."

A greedy spirit often reveals itself when a person has the opportunity to give unselfishly. A man who started with practically nothing committed to give a percentage of his income to God. The first week the man needed to give less than ten dollars because his income didn't reach one hundred dollars.

As time passed, his business prospered. Soon, he was giving almost one thousand dollars a week.

> Only through giving do we learn to have an unselfish spirit.

The now-successful businessman went back to his pastor and said, "I stated that if God would bless me I would give him a percentage, but I didn't know my business would do as well as it has done. How can I get released from that promise?" The pastor thought for a moment and said, "I don't think you can be released from your promise, so why don't we get on our knees like we did before? This time, let's ask God to shrink your income so you can afford to give only one dollar a week."

What we give is not nearly as important as how we live, but the manner in which we live is often governed by how we give. If we're under grace, we should learn the art of joyful giving—not what we're required to give but what we're inspired to give.

During the reign of Alexander the Great, a beggar approached the emperor. Alexander reached into a small bag and gave the beggar some gold coins. An aide to Alexander was startled by the generosity of the gift and said, "Sir, you've given this beggar gold coins when simple copper would have been sufficient." The emperor replied, "Copper would surely have suited the beggar's need, but gold suits Alexander's giving."

What we leave behind is more than money and possessions. We also leave behind a legacy that includes the spirit in which we gave.

QUESTIONS FOR REFLECTION AND DISCUSSION

1. What can we learn in Proverbs 6:1–5 about borrowing money and going into debt?

2. In your opinion, what is the most important reason for giving for a person of faith?

3. What do you think the author means by "the art of joyful giving"?

4. Why are money and giving such sensitive, controversial subjects for most people?

5. Why is it important that we learn how to manage and protect our financial assets?

21

HOW WILL YOU
BE REMEMBERED?

My FAVORITE EPITAPH is the one that says, "I told you I was sick!"

Many years ago, a journalism student working on a college newspaper was conducting an interview with me. She surprised me with her question: "What would you like inscribed on your tombstone?" At the time, I had not yet turned forty, and I was somewhat taken aback by that question. I don't remember exactly what I said in response, but I do remember fumbling about for an answer and attempting to mask my unease with thinking about something so terminal as my tombstone. Since that time, I've had a chance to think about a more thoughtful response to the question.

The kind of legacy we leave is tied directly to the kind of life we live. The fruit of the tree will always bear a genetic relationship to the root of the tree. A life that was lived selfishly and carelessly will not blossom forth into something dramatically different when it ends. The kernel of corn produces corn. The tomato seed produces a tomato plant and more tomatoes. A grain of wheat has the capacity to produce only more wheat.

The life of a caring, loving, hardworking, generous person will leave a much different mark than that of a person who spoke ill of others, was manipulative, thoughtless, cruel, and hoarded everything he had. One thing is certain: When it comes to material things, we'll leave it all. There's no "carry forward" of property when it comes to the afterlife. The only treasure that can be sent ahead is the treasure of the soul.

Three Possible Ways
We Will Be Remembered

In the end, it's not the amount of cash we have but the level of character we possess that determines how we will be remembered and how we'll live in the next life that God has prepared. There are three distinct possibilities.

Unprepared (Rare)

Pity the person who spends a lifetime seeking to be famous and wealthy, achieves these goals, and in the end has nothing else to show for his life. It reminds us of the man Jesus spoke of in Luke 12:20. The man had accumulated great wealth, but God said to him, "You fool! This very night your life will be demanded from you. Then who will get what you have prepared for yourself?"

There are many people whose lives revolve around stock splits, economic expansions, recessions, inflation numbers, and employment figures. But they're not prepared for the conclusion of life and the beginning of eternity.

Rising to the Highest Level of Mediocrity (Medium)

Someone said that the person who seeks to travel in the middle of the road today will be roadkill tomorrow. On some things we can't be both for and against, hot and cold, up and down, north and south. We have to take a stand.

It's tempting to try to live in such a way that we offend no one and please everyone. But the person going down the center line meets only oncoming traffic.

At some point in life, we must decide whether we believe in God and where that belief will take us. We have to move past the notion that we can make everyone happy. We must get over the fact that we cannot accept all things as true. We cannot place our faith in the Jesus of the Bible and put our faith in the innate goodness of humanity at the same time.

> At some point in life, we must decide whether we believe in God and where that belief will take us.

It is sad to think of a person who lives life so unprepared that he ignores what happens when the curtain closes. It's equally sad when someone believes it's possible to accept everything, believe everything, and embrace everything that has been put forth about the ultimate destination of the human spirit. If God did become a person, live on earth in the form of Jesus, die, rise from the grave to conquer death, and invite us to share eternal life with him, then that will be proved at death.

I can't say with personal authority what will happen to a person who travels the path I've chosen. I only must be certain the path I've chosen will lead me to the life beyond that corresponds to my life below.

Done Well (Fully Cooked)

I've thought a lot in recent years about what I hope will be said of me and carved into my tombstone once my physical body turns to dust while my spirit soars to God. In speeches I often say, "I've learned not to live for the weekend or the next event or the next election but rather to live for the next lifetime."

If at the conclusion of my tenure on earth I could hear six words uttered by my Creator, I would feel I had crossed the finish line, breaking the tape with my chest and achieving the championship. These six words can shape our decisions, guide our activities, and help us establish our priorities. They can change our relationship with God and our relationships with others. More than I hope to have kind words written about me in the newspaper or to be mentioned as a footnote in our state's history, I hope that when my life's journey is over, I'll hear these six words: "Well done, good and faithful servant!" (Matthew 25:23).

That's it. That's what I want to hear—six words worth living for and dying for. Rather than being noted for some singular earthly achievement, I would rather the totality of my life be evaluated. I hope not to be seen as some raw and unprepared dish that held great promise but was never fully cooked. Neither do I want my life to be something that appears finished on the outside but inside is still raw from never having the core inner values brought to maturity.

I would hope my life would be full and complete. I want my life to be done well. And I hope that someday it will be said of me, "Well done, good and faithful servant!"

QUESTIONS FOR REFLECTION AND DISCUSSION

1. Have you thought about what you would like inscribed on your tombstone? What features of your life will likely be remembered after you are gone?

2. What do you think the author means by this statement: "The only treasure that can be sent ahead is the treasure of the soul"?

3. How should a person get prepared for the conclusion of life and the beginning of eternity?

4. If you were to evaluate your life right now, would you say you are living a life that is rare, medium, or done well?

5. What actions and behaviors are you demonstrating today that are leading toward this ultimate evaluation by the Master: "Well done, good and faithful servant!" (Matthew 25:23)?

"Keep Your Fork!"

A WOMAN HAD BEEN DIAGNOSED with a terminal illness and given three months to live. As she was getting her things in order, she discussed her final wishes with her pastor. She told him the songs she wanted sung at her funeral, the Scriptures she wanted him to read, and the outfit she wanted to be buried in. The woman also asked to be buried with her favorite Bible.

As the pastor was preparing to leave, the woman remembered something very important to her. "There's one more thing," she said excitedly.

"What's that?" came the pastor's reply.

"This is very important," the woman continued. "I want to be buried with a fork in my right hand."

The pastor stood looking at the woman, not knowing quite what to say.

"That surprises you, doesn't it?" the woman asked.

"Well, to be honest, I'm puzzled by your request," said the pastor.

The woman explained. "In all my years of attending church socials and potluck dinners, I remember that when the dishes of the main course were being cleared, someone would inevitably lean over and say, 'Keep your fork.' That was my favorite part, because I knew that something better was coming—like velvety chocolate cake or deep-dish apple pie. Something wonderful, and with substance!

"So I want people to see me there in that casket with a fork in my hand, and I want them to wonder, *What's with the fork?* Then I want you to tell them, 'Keep the fork! The best is yet to come!'"

The pastor's eyes welled up with tears of joy as he hugged the woman good-bye. He knew this would be one of the last times he would see her before her death. But he also knew that the woman had a better grasp of heaven than he did. She knew that something better was coming.

During the viewing at the funeral home, people walked by the woman's casket and saw the pretty dress she was wearing and her favorite Bible and the fork placed in her right hand. Over and over the pastor heard the question, "What's with the fork?" And over and over he smiled.

During his message in the funeral service that followed, the pastor told the people about the conversation he had with the woman shortly before she died. He also told them about the fork and what it symbolized to her. The pastor told the people how he could not stop thinking about the fork and told them that they probably would not be able to stop thinking about it either. He was right.

So, the next time you reach down for your fork, let it remind you—oh so gently—that the best is yet to come.

Notes

Chapter 1: Living Happily Ever After

1. Les Carpenter, "Aaron Hernandez Died As He Lived: A Mystery to Everyone," *The Guardian,* US Edition, April 19, 2017, https://www.theguardian.com/sport/blog/2017/apr/19/aaron-hernandez -death-prison-nfl.

Chapter 5: Families in Freefall

1. Centers for Disease Control and Prevention, National Center for Health Statistics. *National Vital Statistics Reports.* "Divorce rates by State: 1990, 1995, and 1999-2014." https://www.cdc .gov/nchs/data/dvs/state_divorce_rates_90_95_and_99-14.pdf.

Chapter 6: From Love to Lust

1. Luke Gilkerson, "How Many Women Are Hooked on Porn? 10 Stats That May Shock You," Covenant Eyes, August 30, 2013, http://www.covenanteyes.com/2013/08/30/women -addicted-to-porn-stats/.

Chapter 7: Parents Do Matter

1. Mike Huckabee and George Grant, *Kids Who Kill: Confronting Our Culture of Violence* (Nashville: B&H, 1998).

Chapter 13: The Power of Being Positive

1. "Bickering Mars the A.T.&T. Annual Meeting; 2-1 Stock Split Is Voted—Bid for Billy Rose Fails," *New York Times,* April 16, 1964, https://www.nytimes.com/1964/04/16/archives/bickering-mars -the-att-annual-meeting-21-stock-split-is-voted-bid.html.

2. Chérie Carter-Scott, *Negaholics: How to Overcome Negativity and Turn Your Life Around* (New York: Ballantine, 1999).

3. *Journal of the American Medical Association,* "Humor Therapy: Relieving Chronic Pain and Enhancing Happiness for Older Adults," June 28, 2010, https://www.ncbi.nlm.nih.gov/pmc /articles/PMC2989702/.

4. E. Hansen, K.T. Gundersen, and S. Svebak, "Sense of Humor and General Life Satisfaction in Association with the Biological Effects of Resistance Training in People with Impaired Glucose Tolerance," *Health* 9, no. 5 (2017): 870–82, https://doi.org/10.4236/health.2017.95062.

5. Angela Haupt, "How Your Personality Affects Your Health," *US News & World Report,* September 22, 2010, https://health.usnews.com/health-news/family-health/heart/articles /2010/09/22/how-your-personality-affects-your-health.

Chapter 14: It's the Money, Honey

1. James Strong, *Strong's Exhaustive Concordance of the Bible,* updated ed. (Peabody, MA: Hendrickson Publishers, 2007), 1566.

Chapter 15: Using What You Have

1. Corrie ten Boom, *The Hiding Place*, 35th anniversary ed. (Grand Rapids: Chosen Books, 2006), 44.

Chapter 19: Toward the Exit Sign

1. Elisabeth Kübler-Ross, *On Death and Dying* (New York: Macmillan, 1969).

About the Author

MIKE HUCKABEE served as the governor of Arkansas from 1996–2007 and is a former presidential candidate. Before entering politics in 1992, he was in broadcasting and advertising and then worked for twelve years as a full-time pastor and denominational leader. Mike currently is the host of the TBN weekend show "Huckabee" and is a frequent Fox News contributor. Mike is considered a top TV personality and social media influencer. He is the best-selling author of twelve books, including, *God, Guns, Grits, and Gravy; Dear Chandler, Dear Scarlett; A Simple Government; Do the Right Thing;* and *From Hope to Higher Ground.* Mike's commentary is read every day and he is a frequent speaker around the world. He also has ownership interest in radio stations across several states. He has been married to Janet since 1974 and they have three adult children and six grandchildren. They live in Florida but maintain close ties to their native home in Arkansas.

IF YOU ENJOYED THIS BOOK, WILL YOU CONSIDER SHARING THE MESSAGE WITH OTHERS?

Mention the book in a blog post or through Facebook, Twitter, Pinterest, or upload a picture through Instagram.

Recommend this book to those in your small group, book club, workplace, and classes.

Head over to facebook.com/mikehuckabee, "LIKE" the page, and post a comment as to what you enjoyed the most.

Tweet "I recommend reading #RareMediumOrDoneWell by @GovMikeHuckabee?lang=en // @worthypub"

Pick up a copy for someone you know who would be challenged and encouraged by this message.

Write a book review online.

Visit us at worthypublishing.com

twitter.com/worthypub

worthypub.tumblr.com

facebook.com/worthypublishing

pinterest.com/worthypub

instagram.com/worthypub

youtube.com/worthypublishing